# MARRIED
## WITH CHILDREN

_Ed O'Neill_

_Katey Sagal_

_Christina Applegate_

_David Faustino_

_Amanda Bearse_

# PIG OUT WITH PEG

☆ ☆ ☆ ☆ ☆ ☆

## SECRETS FROM
## THE BUNDY FAMILY KITCHEN

by

# Peg Bundy

as told to
**Linda Merinoff**

AVON BOOKS ▲ NEW YORK

AVON BOOKS
A division of
The Hearst Corporation
105 Madison Avenue
New York, New York 10016

Copyright © 1990 by ELP Communications
Text design by Levavi and Levavi
Published by arrangement with Columbia Pictures Merchandising
ISBN: 0-380-76431-8

First Avon Books Trade Printing: November 1990

AVON TRADEMARK REG. U.S. PAT. OFF. AND IN OTHER COUNTRIES, MARCA REGISTRADA, HECHO EN U.S.A.

Printed in the U.S.A.

RA   10   9   8   7   6   5   4   3   2   1

# Contents

> *"In the history of the Bundy family, no wife has ever worked inside or outside the home."* —Peg

# A VERY PERSONAL NOTE FROM PEG

If you know Peg Bundy, you know I stand for something aside from using my husband's hopes and dreams for a Handi-Wipe. Hey, this is *important,* so put down the cheesecake and diet soda and listen.

I say why should women age and sweat and die early? That's what husbands and kids are for. Come on, girls. Take a stand. Every hour you watch daytime television is a blow for freedom. Every minute you vacuum shoves you farther into homemaker hell.

But sometimes life isn't perfect. No matter how hard you kick, you scream, you dig in your spike heels, the day's going to come when you can't hold out against the final degradation.

Yes, ladies, you're going to have to *cook* for your family. Maybe it's the day they disconnect your phone, or the board of health finally closes your local fast-food joint for good, or your family says they won't be home till late and they suddenly show up and catch you baking yourself a chocolate Bundt cake.

The point is your family's finally going to find out you *can* put something in the oven besides your head and last night's dirty dishes.

Don't get me wrong—food is O.K. in its place, but not when you have to work at it. That's where I can help you. The recipes in this book are the closest thing to not cooking and still putting edible food on the table.

Hey, I know you don't need another cookbook telling you how to stuff rice into peas. I don't read cookbooks myself. Well, I did buy *Joy of Cooking* once, but I thought it was *Joy of Sex*. That was before I met Al and found out that Joy was something that came in a squeeze bottle.

Why am I doing womankind this favor? For the only reason a woman should ever lift a finger. Yeah, for the money. God, this is embarrassing—a real woman swipes enough from her husband's pants to buy anything she needs and banks $5,000 a year.

But I'm in big trouble. I suddenly realized that Al already looks so awful, how will I know when he's about to kick off? Sure he'll be smiling, but by then it will be too late. No husband, no money. So, I jumped into action.

I'm very proud of this book. It's flashy, it's exciting, it's easy. Yes—it's me! Here are great-tasting recipes you can serve to your family, company, perfect strangers, escaped felons, even rich doctors. So do us both a favor and buy it before you're picked up for loitering.

Oh yes, in case you're wondering what I'm going to do when my family reads this and finds out I can really cook—get real, this is after all a *book*! And besides, I found a really great place to hide it.

Peg Bundy
*Chicago, Illinois*
*MARCH, 1990*

**Any resemblance
to recipes living or dead
is purely coincidental.**

*"I had a rough day, and all I want is some peace, a meal, and some hemlock. Is that too much to ask?"—Al*

# "Yeah, I Found the Book"
# by Al

That Peg is such a great little housekeeper. When I found this book hidden in the broom closet under Peg's dust collection and a stack of old *Playboy*s, I was so desperate for food I almost ate it. And then it hit me. I was so stunned, I forgot I was looking for some rope and a stool—Peg had actually been in the broom closet!

Believe it or not, I was once a man with hopes and dreams and money for a phone call. When a guy gets married, he expects regular sex and regular meals. Well, all he wants is the meals, but he's willing to pay the price. But when he doesn't get any food at all and spends sixty hours a week selling shoes so the wife won't have to give up her Gold Card, something's got to go. I think it's the sex, don't you? Try and tell that to Peg. It's a nightly battle of wills—Peg keeps asking me if I've made mine.

But I wasn't really surprised when I found the cookbook. Food plays a big part in our marital bliss. Peg knows how to keep me on my toes. What can you say about a woman who goes to the trouble of making hash blacks to go with your bagels and Maalox? She's especially popular with Chicago's Engine Co. #9—they always show up for her Southern fried chicken or, as they call it, Mississippi Burning.

You've got to hand it to Peg, though. (No, actually, you don't; she usually just reaches in and grabs it.) She's real good about not cooking that woman food—consomme, crepes, pate, the stuff with accents over the e's. But she sure knows her fancy food. Until I met her, I thought an aspic was something you used when your Preparation H didn't work.

So now, lucky reader (I call you that since you don't actually live with us), you have but to turn the page to enjoy all those great dishes Peg never makes for us. But I've got to be going now. I see Peg's picking up her favorite utensil, the old melon de-baller. . . .

# INTRODUCTION

*"Would you like me to make you some soup for your lunch tomorrow, Al?"*

*"No, Peg, it's O.K. . . . last time I cut my lip on the can."*

# How to Be the Perfect Housewife

Everybody asks how I do it—take care of a husband and two kids, keep the house looking perfect and still have time to cook those great meals. Well, I'm not going to pretend it's easy. . . . I'm not even going to pretend I do it. Work is stupid. As Mom always says, "Never feed a man when you can feed yourself twice."

Don't be afraid to take advantage of your kids. When Bud and Kelly were young, I used to make housework a game. Whoever did the most work got to eat dinner that night! Now that they've worked off most of that baby fat, it's a little harder.

Kelly won't make the beds anymore. She says she's seen enough beds to last her a lifetime. But she always seems to have more money and jewelry than the rest of us, so I guess I don't have to worry about her. Bud still takes out the garbage . . . and helps himself to a bedtime snack at the same time. I have to pay him too, but luckily he'll still take Al's old *Playboy*s instead of money.

When I need Al's help around the house, I just tell him it's that or sex. Last time I looked, he was still frantically buffing the bathroom grout with his fingernails.

1

*"Hey, Peg, what's for breakfast?"*

*"Nothing, Al."*

*"We had that yesterday, but you sure know how to make it."*

# It's the Big Building with the Food in It

Let's face it, grocery shopping is your toughest job. How do you feed a family of four on $26.50 a week and still manage to keep $25.00 of that for yourself? The best way is not to go shopping at all. If your husband and kids ask you where dinner is, tell them it's at the store.

Of course you need to go to the market once a week for the *Enquirer, The Globe,* and *The Star,* so you might as well pick up a little something while you're there. Don't forget, you've got to eat too. Follow these rules and food shopping will be as painless as possible.

Never patronize stores where you have to wait in line. *Your* time is valuable. Besides, those game shows and soaps cost millions to produce. The least you can do is be home to watch them.

TV also helps you keep up on consumer issues. The moment Meryl Streep starts harping about pesticides in honeydew, rush out to the market. The lines in the produce department will be shorter and the people who work there will be nicer to you. By that time, they'll practically be giving the stuff away.

If you need something special, don't just sit around waiting for it to get polluted—phone the alarm in to the tabloids yourself! Beef-hormone scare? Great! I buy extra—with Al, it could only help. Food grown near nuclear power plants (especially one with a recent accident), product tampering, unlicensed cheese factories, and salmonella scares cry out to the alert shopper.

Here's a high-tech tip: Send over one of your kids (we send Bud—he still looks innocent) to the meat department with a thin, black marker and white correction fluid. The next thing you know, the bar code on a Porterhouse reads like it's chicken backs. And to think Al wanted Bud to take auto repair instead of art class.

Of course food borrowing is even better than food buying. No well-bred, self-respecting neighbor expects you to return the stuff. If they do, throw up on their shoes.

Always observe the cardinal rule: Never, never borrow from cheapskates or you'll end up with house brands. You, your kids, and your dog deserve better. And never lend anything to anyone. That kind of thing can break up a friendship.

Reminder: Always keep a container of curdled milk in the fridge in case someone tries to take advantage of your good nature. Then ask them to hold the milk so you can get to what they want. They'll suddenly remember the all-night Pic & Eat in Skokie.

> *"Well, if someone is going to be doing some work in the kitchen, I guess I'd better go upstairs and rest."*—Peg

# The Perfect Equipment for the Perfect Kitchen

When Al and I first went looking for a house, there were only two we could afford. I wanted the adorable one without the kitchen. So when Al put his foot down and insisted on the other, I was deeply touched. I pictured delicious hot breakfasts, saucy sandwiches for lunch, and gourmet dinners. Then I found out he wasn't planning on doing the cooking.

As long as you're stuck with a kitchen, you might as well stock it with the right appliances. First, you need a good cooking timer to tell you when to phone Domino's Pizza—they deliver.

Second, a broken toaster-oven painted to look like a microwave so people won't know how poor your husband really is.

Third, a pop-up toaster for burgers and frozen fries.

O.K., ladies, enough theory. Now let's get to the gruesome details.

# THE RECIPES

> *"Mom, we're starving. Feed us or trade us."—Bud*

## Family Cooking: Give Us This Day Our Bundy Bread

I know I talk a lot about looking after number one, but how can you respect yourself if you don't take care of your family too? Well, I can live with it. Why can't you?

Sometimes, though, an assassination or something preempts your soaps, so why not devote those few minutes to your loved ones? Don't worry—it's not like you planned to waste the time.

O.K., you've only got an hour before "Wheel of Fortune." So how do you keep your family happy and healthy enough to fool a nearsighted caseworker a couple of times a month? Here's the Peg Bundy method, perfected by years of practice.

A BALANCED DIET is very important. That's why each dish I serve must have at least two basic ingredients. I know vegetables taste awful, but your local 7-Eleven is filled with veggies your kids will love, like Vegetable Thins crackers, corn curls, potato chips, guacomole bean dip, microwave popcorn, and Dr. Brown's original Cel-Ray Tonic.

FIBER is also real important, but so many of those new products

5

are expensive. Do you have any idea what Tim Conway and Harvey Korman get for one lousy commercial? So make your own Fruit and Fibre cereal by topping SmurfBerry Crunch with unpeeled banana slices.

If your kids demand hot cereal, just tell them to wait until you've scraped the oatmeal scrub off your face. It only takes a minute to heat it up. Face your kids with clear skin and a clear conscience!

IMPROVISATION is the key to great family meals. If the kids want alphabet soup, chop up last night's noodles and tell them it's Arabic. (Actually, real Arabic alphabet soup is usually pretty cheap when you can find it—and Al loves that camel broth.)

If your husband says he wants a hot meal or he'll cancel his life insurance, stick an open can of tuna topped with Miracle Whip and breadcrumbs under the broiler. If you've got guests, take the label off the can.

And never admit there's no food in the house. Simply drag a piece of stale white bread through an empty Tang jar and voilà— Tang Wipes, a Bundy tradition.

SPECIAL FAMILY OCCASIONS really bring out the wife and mother in me. It makes me so proud to see their happy faces when they know I've gone that extra mile—but then there's no Pup & Taco in the neighborhood, so I don't have much of a choice.

SCHOOL LUNCHES are important. I always try to pack something nutritious and tasty for Bud and Kelly. A dollar and a map to Burger King seems to make everyone happy.

Don't be too extravagant, though. Once you start doing things for your family, they never give you a moment's peace. It's "Mom, cook me breakfast," "Mom, pack me a sandwich," "Peg, pack me a suitcase," every damn month!

And it gets even worse—once you start feeding them regularly, it won't be long before you start asking how they're doing in school . . . or even letting them go to the doctor when they're sick.

I'd love to tell you that the following recipes are tried and true Bundy favorites, but of course, they're not. They're tried and true *Peg* Bundy favorites that usually disappear before anyone else gets home.

## SMOKE ALARM STEAK

Why do I call this Smoke Alarm Steak? Because, Einstein, I cook it until the smoke alarm goes off. So if your family doesn't know you're cooking—and why would they think you were?—they'll think the house is on fire and you'll get to eat this all by yourself. (Serves them right for locking the door on the way out.)

Actually, it is recommended that you do this cooking outside.

Plan ahead to get high-quality meat. I find out where our neighbors Steve and Marcy are going to dinner, then call ahead and order a blood-rare chateaubriand for two. They're vegetarians—but they're too spineless to stand up to the waiter, so they'll bring it back for our dog, Buck. Unfortunately, you really can't do this too often—about every six weeks seems to be the limit.

> 2 teaspoons garlic salt
> 1 teaspoon black pepper
> 2 teaspoons dry mustard
> 1 teaspoon cayenne
> ½ teaspoon dried thyme leaves
> 1 teaspoon ground cardamom
> 1½ teaspoons ground cumin
> 1 double or 2 single very rare steak(s), 1½
>     pounds total before cooking

Put a 9″ or 10″ cast-iron skillet over the highest flame you've got and heat it until it's smoking and the bottom is turning white. Mix together everything but the steak on a dinner plate. Lay the steak on the spices, then turn it over. Pat the spices into both sides of the steak in an even layer. Carefully lay the steak in the skillet, preferably with tongs, and cook until the bottom is blackened. Turn it over and cook the other side until blackened or the smoke alarm sounds. *Caution:* The house may really be on fire. Better check.

*Serves 2 people (if you screw up).*

# A GOOD HOT LUNCH

Kids are so damn insecure. Sometimes they ask you to do the craziest things to prove you love them. Would you believe, the other day Bud and Kelly begged me to fix them—are you ready?—a nourishing hot lunch? Where do they get ideas like that? Certainly not at home! It just goes to show—you do your best to try to protect them from bad influences and they still break your heart.

What could I do? I threw this together and told them it was a hot turkey sandwich with mashed potatoes and gravy. Since this was their first hot lunch, they never knew the difference.

> *4 slices angel food cake, each cut ½" thick*
> *2 cups apple pie filling, canned or (yeah, right)*
> *homemade (page 70)*
> *2 scoops vanilla ice cream*
> *Warm butterscotch sauce, bought or (ditto)*
> *homemade (next recipe)*

Toast the cake slices till they're light brown all over. Take two plates and put a slice on each. Spoon on the apples and cover with the unused slices so they look like sandwiches. Cut them in half and stick a frilly toothpick in each half. Put a scoop of ice cream on each plate and pour on the butterscotch sauce.

*Serves 2 gullible kids.*

# HOMEMADE BUTTERSCOTCH SAUCE

This is so easy, even Kelly could make it. But if you still think you need a friend to help you with the tough parts, pick a diabetic so you won't have to share it. Nothing beats watching "Win, Lose or Draw" with a bag of pretzels and a big bowl of homemade butterscotch sauce for dipping.

I love this sauce. I love it on pies, I love it on puddings, I love it on French toast, I love it on ice cream. I love the way a bowl of it on the coffee table catches bugs before they fly into Al's mouth.

And if you have company, it makes a great fondue! Use fruit, though, instead of bread or beef.

> *1 cup light brown sugar*
> *3 tablespoons unsalted butter*
>   *Pinch of salt*
> *½ cup light corn syrup*
> *½ cup heavy cream*

Throw everything but the cream into a small saucepan and turn the heat to medium. Bring it to a boil. You only have to stir till the sugar's dissolved and the butter's melted, then you can smoke a cigarette. When it begins boiling, begin timing 5 minutes.

You know it's ready when it's smooth, thick, and frothy, and you can pick some up with a spoon, drop it into a bowl of cold water and roll it into a soft little ball. Take the pan off the heat and beat in the cream. You can serve it at any temperature, but the cooler it gets, the thicker it gets.

*Makes 1½ cups.*

## CHERNOBYL CHICKEN MELTDOWN SANDWICH

Your family never appreciates the trouble you go to for them. You feed a family of four for $0.64 and all you hear is "Mom, why does this chicken have three legs" and "Peg, didn't you think just maybe there was something wrong when the label said Chernobyl Farms?" Well, excuse me for thinking of our bank book.

Of course you can't find Chernobyl Farms chicken at your local market anymore, thanks to those know-it-alls in Washington, but don't give up hope. Check meat packages for those little signs—a flipper, a lump of unidentifiable tissue, a hospital bracelet. It's worth it. A meal like this teaches the kids an unforgettable lesson in the twin dangers of atomic power and eating at home.

*3 cooked chicken legs*
*5 tablespoons barbecue sauce*
*4 slices Russian rye bread*
*6 tablespoons sour cream*
  *"Hot Mexican" Velveeta*

Remove the meat from the chicken legs in bite-size pieces, if you didn't buy ones with the meat falling off already. Shield each piece with barbecue sauce so your family doesn't notice the glow. Char the bread lightly in the toaster. Blanket each slice of bread with ¼ of the chicken mixture and enshroud with 1½ tablespoons of the sour cream. Bury under sliced Velveeta. Put under the broiler till the cheese is bubbly and spotted with radiation burns.

*Serves 4 people.*

## MEAL-IN-A-CONE

You know how some days you don't feel like convincing the kids to wash the dishes? You've run out of Chinet. Your husband put his foot down and won't let you use his high school football plaques anymore. And somebody forgot to empty the ashtrays, again. Great. Now what are you going to do for plates? And forget forks—who can afford plastic these days?

   Well, don't say I never did anything for you. Here's the Peg Bundy solution to all your problems. Well, except for the fact that you're sitting there reading a cookbook.

*4 tablespoons unsalted butter*
*2 tablespoons + 2 teaspoons unsweetened*
  *cocoa powder*
*⅔ cup pre-sifted flour (you don't expect me to*
  *sift my own flour, do you?)*
*¼ teaspoon baking soda*
  *Pinch of salt*
*6 tablespoons milk*
*½ teaspoon vanilla extract*
*½ cup sugar*
*2 large egg yolks*
*8 cake ice cream cones with flat bottoms*
*8 gingersnaps or any other cookie which fits*
  *snugly inside the cone halfway down*
*1 recipe tuna salad (next recipe)*

Turn on the TV. As soon as Oprah starts strutting her new thin-clothes, begin measuring out the ingredients. While she denies the latest rumor about her sex life, turn the oven to 350 degrees. During the first commercial break, melt the butter. In the time it takes to introduce today's tragic crime victim, mix together the cocoa, flour, baking soda, and salt.

During the second commercial break you'll have enough time to mix together the milk, melted butter, vanilla, sugar, and egg yolks, stir the flour mixture into the milk mixture until it's smooth.

As soon as the guest begins to cry, set the cones on a baking sheet. As soon as Oprah begins to cry, hold a spoonful of batter slightly above the cone and directly over the center. Push it off the spoon with your finger, so that it falls to the bottom of the cone without hitting the sides. This can be tricky and you may even have to take your eyes off the TV. Use about 2½ tablespoons of batter per cone. If some gets stuck on the sides of the cone, push it down with a damp tiny spoon.

When Oprah reaches the guest's assailant on the prison phone, put the cupcakes in the oven. While he's apologizing to his victim and explaining how pornography made him the scum he is today, bake the cones. Be sure not to burn them if he's still apologizing—they only take about 30 minutes. A skewer inserted into the cupcake should come out clean around the time someone in the audience recommends putting a skewer through the guy's heart.

Cool the cupcakes until the prisoner asks for his victim's address so he can thank her personally for forgiving him. Then, as the credits roll, cut the tops off the cupcakes to make them flat. Eat the tops or put lard between them and tell the kids they're sandwich cookies.

Just before you're ready to serve the cones, wedge the cookies in. Add a scoop of tuna salad on top and eat right away.

*Makes 8 cupcakes.*

## TUNA SALAD

> 2 tablespoons tiny black raisins or currants
>   Rum
> 1 can (6½ ounces) oil-packed tuna, white if you
>     can afford it
> ¼ cup chopped celery
> 2 tablespoons minced onion
> ¼ cup mayonnaise
> 1 teaspoon prepared horseradish
> 1 tablespoon prepared mustard

Put the raisins in a small bowl and pour on enough rum to cover them completely. Soak them overnight, then pat them dry. All that work to put a little life into something so small and shriveled—but I guess I'm used to that. Drink the rum or pour it back into the bottle.

Drain the tuna and mash it in a bowl. Stir in the raisins, celery, and onion. Beat the mayonnaise, horseradish, and mustard together until they're smooth, then stir them into the tuna.

## PAN PANCAKES

If your family expects you to slave over a hot stove flipping pancake after pancake like some brain-dead fry cook, they're crazy. Pour that batter into a pan, shove it in the oven, and grab that copy of the *Star* to see whose maracas Roseanne Barr busted this week.

Now I suppose you're going to say where am I going to get *two* frying pans? No problem. Tell your neighbors you're recycling scrap metal because you need the money to get your husband a vasectomy. Suburban types are suckers for anything that has recycling in it—you can steal them blind. Mention the ozone layer and they'll positively beg you to car-pool with them.

> *1½ cups pre-sifted flour*
> *1½ teaspoons ground cinnamon*
> *1 teaspoon ground nutmeg*
> *¼ teaspoon salt*
> *6 large eggs*
> *1½ cups milk*
> *6 tablespoons unsalted butter, chopped into*
>    *small bits*
>    *Confectioners' sugar*
>    *Frozen strawberries, thawed, with their*
>    *syrup*

Turn the oven to 425 degrees. Put two 9″ ovenproof skillets, preferably cast-iron, in the oven. Mix the flour, cinnamon, nutmeg, and salt in a bowl. Stir the eggs and mix together until the yolks are broken up, then pour them into the flour bowl. Stir with a fork just until there are no more white streaks or balls. The great thing about using a fork is it's real hard to overbeat something even if you're crazy enough to try.

Put half the butter into each skillet, then swirl the pans around so the butter covers the bottom. Pour half the batter into each pan and put them in the oven. Bake about 20 minutes, until they're puffed and golden—like giant alien mushrooms—with very brown edges.

Take the pans out of the oven and bring them to the table. Sprinkle the pancakes with confectioners' sugar, then cut each one in half and serve. Use small plates so the portions look larger. If the kids get up early enough and your neighbors' fruit trees are in season, top the pancakes with sliced fresh fruit. Otherwise you're stuck with the frozen strawberries.

*Serves 4 people.*

## HASH STUFFED PEPPERS

Al really hates green peppers, so I try to make them at least once a week. My friend Marcy says she once was served hash in a fancy New York restaurant, but I think she had one Harvey Wallbanger too many. Let's face it, hash looks like pig food. I know, I know, now you're going to ask me why I bother to make my own hash. There's a very good reason. I suddenly went insane one day, and the next thing I knew, there it was.

> *2½ cans (15½-ounce size) corned beef hash or 1*
> *recipe homemade (next recipe)*
> *If you're using canned hash:*
> *3 teaspoons Worcestershire sauce*
> *2 tablespoons heavy cream*
> *1 tablespoon unsalted butter*
> *Couple of dashes of Tabasco sauce*
> *4 green peppers, cut in half through the stem*
> *Handful of potato chips or tortilla chips*
> *1 large jar tomato sauce*

Preheat the oven to 375 degrees. Cut off each pepper's stem and scoop out the seeds and the white stuff. Put them in a bowl and tell the family it's salad.

Put a large pot of water on a burner and turn on the heat. Go ahead, be June Cleaver, make the homemade hash—or be you and mix the canned hash, Worcestershire sauce, heavy cream, butter, and Tabasco sauce together in a shallow, wide baking dish. Put either hash in the oven and bake it 25 minutes. If you plan on eating some of it yourself, you've really got to stir this well after the first 15 minutes.

While the hash is baking, drop the pepper halves in the boiling water. You could burn yourself when the water splashes, so have one of the kids do it. Boil 5 minutes, then drain them, cut side down, on paper towels. You could burn yourself taking them out of the pot, so have one of the kids do this too. You may have to use a different kid this time.

Put the chips in a reclosable plastic bag and seal it. Put the bag under the couch cushions just before the sports news comes on. Five minutes later when the financial segment starts, Al will get depressed and wander off, and you can retrieve them. If absolutely necessary, you can crush the bag with your hands, but if you have to resort to that you've been missing the point.

Don't bother turning the oven off when you take the hash out. Stuff it into the pepper halves. Pat the chips onto the hash. Put the peppers in one or two baking dishes large enough to hold them in one layer. It's O.K. if the peppers touch each other slightly. Pour tomato sauce around the peppers until it's 1" deep. Bake 15 minutes.

*Serves 4 people.*

## HOMEMADE CORNED BEEF HASH

You don't have to stuff this into peppers—you can stuff it into your face. Just bake it for 25 minutes at 375 degrees, stirring it halfway through, so more of it gets crusty.

> 1¼ pounds cooked corned beef, finely chopped
>       or coarsely ground
> 1 cup finely chopped onion
> 3½ cups cooked potato, cut into tiny little cubes
> ¼ cup melted unsalted butter
> 2 garlic cloves, finely minced or crushed with a
>       hammer
> 2 tablespoons heavy cream
> 2 teaspoons Worcestershire sauce
>       Couple of dashes of Tabasco sauce

Toss everything together in a wide shallow baking dish.

# LEFTOVER SALAD SOUP

In our house, all salad is leftover salad—who wants to eat that stuff? If your family hates vegetables as much as they should, just tell them it's this or broccoli. If they've really made you mad, it's this and broccoli.

You should serve soup as often as possible. It's good for your family and it's good for you—nobody'll notice if you don't use clean bowls.

> *6 slices of bacon*
> *2 scallions, white and light green sections*
> *    only, roughly chopped*
> *1 large baking potato, roughly chopped*
> *2 cups chicken broth*
> *2–3 cups green salad with dressing*

Cut the bacon into 1″ pieces with a pair of scissors. I use Al's nose clippers and the next morning he always says how easily they go in. Of course there's always the chance they'll slide into his brain, but who'd notice? Cook the bacon in a big soup pot over medium heat until the pieces begin to curl.

Turn the heat to low, add the scallions, and stir once in a while for about 10 minutes. Stir in the potatoes, then pour in the broth. Stir again and bring to a boil over high heat. Don't cover the pot or icky frothy stuff from the potatoes will overflow and you'll actually have to clean your stove.

Turn the heat down as low as possible and cook 10–15 minutes, depending on the size of the potato pieces, until a fork will go all the way through one. Pour in the salad, stir well (I never noticed how much stirring there was in this damn recipe before. This is the last time I make it!), and simmer another 10 minutes until the greens are cooked. If you want thicker soup, pour half the pot into a blender or food processor, mash it to a pulp, then pour it back in.

If you're a neat-freak, you can skim some of the fat off the top. You can always use it as hand cream or, if God answers prayers, a lubricant.

*Serves 4 people.*

# PEG IRON CHEESE SANDWICH

If you don't have an iron (congratulations!), you can always drive over the sandwich with your husband's car (if his tires are as bald as he is, they will work just fine). But you'll have to use expensive foil, like Reynolds Wrap Construction Grade. If you want a little more protein, place the sandwich in the path of an ant colony. If you time it just right, you can get the maximum number of ants in the sandwich with the minimum amount of cheese loss. (NOTE: Use studded snow tires for a nice waffling effect.)

> *2 slices white bread*
> *Butter*
> *Velveeta Cheese*

Set your iron to Linen if there's no Cheese setting. Put a slice of bread between two sheets of aluminum foil. Use a rolling pin to get it as flat as possible. Flatten the second piece the same way.

Butter the bread on both sides. Slice just enough Velveeta to make a thin sandwich and put it between the slices of bread. Stick the sandwich back between the sheets of foil. Iron for about a minute, 30 seconds each side, checking once to make sure the bread isn't burning. If you want to make sure the iron can never be used for clothes again, forget the foil. Peel and serve.

*Makes 1.*

# ONE-CAN CASSEROLE

You never really appreciate the joys of camping until the bank throws you out of your house. I'm not talking about the palace we live in now. I mean when Al and I first got married and he turned down the Bears contract and went to shoe school. It was either I get a job or we were out on the streets.

The streets aren't so bad if you know how to cook over a trash-can fire. We were camping on the lot where we're living now, when the neighbors chipped in to build a house around us so they wouldn't have to look at us anymore. Every summer, when Al's feet make it impossible to stay inside at night, we relive those happy carefree days.

The last thing you want to do when you're camping is wash dishes. Well, actually, the last thing you want to do is go to the bathroom, but you can't avoid that. For this recipe you don't use any pots or pans or plates. All you need are four one-pound coffee cans, with the paper torn off.

*1/4 cup olive or tasteless vegetable oil*
*4 medium boiling potatoes, sliced pretty thin*
  *Salt and pepper to taste*
*3 cups roughly chopped cabbage*
*3 cups roughly chopped onions*
*2 large red bell peppers, seeded, roughly*
  *chopped*
*2 large or 4 small cucumbers, peeled, thinly*
  *sliced*
*1 pound regular ground beef or anything too*
  *slow to get out of the way*

Light some coals in your barbecue. Coat the insides of the cans with the oil. Layer half a potato in the bottom of each can. Sprinkle with salt and pepper. Mix together the cabbage, onions, and peppers with some salt and pepper, then pack them in on top of the potatoes. Top that with the meat and a little more salt and pepper. Pack in the remaining potatoes, then the cucumbers. Sprinkle with just a bit more salt and pepper. Seal the cans with a folded-over piece of foil, then cut three slits in the foil to release the steam.

When the coals are ready, spread them out so there's a layer only one or two coals deep. Put the cans on the coals, then pack in the rest of the coals around them. Cover the barbecue and cook for 30 minutes. Serve in the cans or, if you're entertaining the Pope, pour them out onto paper plates.

*Makes 4 huge servings.*

## PORK-AT-THE-BOTTOM BREAD CASSEROLE

Didn't you ever sit down to a big Christmas dinner and wish you didn't have to eat the turkey? Didn't you wish you could just pig out on the stuffing? Well, that's exactly what this tastes like—a little pig and a lot of stuffing. You know me—I'm not one to brag. But I think this is the best pork-at-the-bottom bread casserole I've ever tasted.

Use whatever bread you've got, even if it's stale. Anything from Wonder Bread to Aunt Melissa's Super Healthful Whole Wheat Power Breakfast Loaf is fine. Make sure you use cheeses you can taste, not the kind where you can't tell the slices from the paper between them.

*5 or 6 slices of bread*
*1½ pounds pork sausage meat*
*Vegetable oil if necessary*
*1½ cups mixed grated or crumbled cheeses like*
*    cheddar, Swiss, Velveeta, Wispride, or*
*    Danish Blue*
*5 large eggs*
*1 cup milk*
*½ teaspoon salt*
*¼ teaspoon pepper*
*1 tablespoon prepared mustard*

Turn the oven to 350 degrees. Fry the sausage meat, using some oil if it starts to stick to the skillet, until it's crumbled and there's no more red in it. While it's cooking, butter a shallow 9″ or 10″ baking dish and put the bread in, squashing it a little to form just one layer. Use a slotted spoon to move the cooked meat directly from the pan to the baking dish. Mix the cheeses together, then spread half over the sausage. Stir the eggs, milk, salt and pepper, and mustard together until smooth, then pour them into the dish. Scatter the rest of the cheese on top.

Bake about 30 minutes until puffed up and golden like a quiche. Don't let anyone else see it while it's looking like a quiche! Wait a minute or two until it's collapsed like it's supposed to, and then you're safe. Serve hot, cut into wedges.

*Serves 6 people.*

## BRAISED VEAL CHOPS

Sometimes you just have to go all out for the ones you love the most. I don't know when, but sometimes.

> *1 tablespoon unsalted butter*
> *2 tablespoons extra virgin olive oil*
> *2 really good veal chops, each ¾″–1″ thick*
> *2 scallions, white and light green sections only,*
>    *finely chopped*
> *2 garlic cloves, crushed, then minced*
>    *Salt and pepper to taste*
> *¼ teaspoon minced fresh or ½ teaspoon dried*
>    *tarragon*
> *1 teaspoon minced fresh or ½ teaspoon ground*
>    *thyme*
> *¼ cup 1985 Corton-Charlemagne or other ex-*
>    *cellent white Burgundy*
> *1½ tablespoons aged vinegar such as balsamic,*
>    *sherry, or red wine*
>    *Homemade chicken stock*

Heat the butter and oil in a 7″ or 8″ skillet over medium-high heat until the butter's melted. Add the chops and brown one side, which should take about 4 minutes. Turn them over and continue cooking. About 2 minutes later, stir in the scallions and garlic, and cook until the second side of the chop is browned. If the garlic starts browning, turn down the heat. If it burns, throw it out and start over. This has to be perfect.

Sprinkle the contents of the pan with the salt, pepper, tarragon, and thyme. Pour in the wine and vinegar and enough stock to come halfway up the sides of the chops. Bring the liquid to a boil, then turn the heat to low. Cover and cook 10 minutes, then turn the chops, cover again, and cook 10 minutes more. If it burns, throw it out and start over.

Remove the chops from the pan and put them on a heated platter. Cover them with foil to keep them warm and prevent them from drying out. If they dry out, throw them out and start over.

Turn the heat under the pan to high and boil the liquid down until there's only a thin layer left in the pan. Spoon the sauce over the chops. Put one chop on your plate, the other in the dog dish.

*Serves you and your dog.*

When Bud found out I was writing this book—he caught me beating an egg—he wanted to help. I offered to let him write the whole thing, but he wanted half the profits. So we compromised. He contributed a recipe, and I promised not to cook it.

## BUD'S HOOTER PIE

Bud Bundy here, with a gastronomic delight guaranteed to put any woman in the mood. One bite of this, she's putty in your hands. Or vice versa, if you're lucky. This is good, very good, as good as Kelly is if you can believe the bathroom walls. And you can make it for just about the same price.

> *1 graham cracker pie crust*
> *3 ounces really great dark chocolate*
> *1 large egg + 1 yolk*
> *1 tablespoon strong coffee*
> *2 tablespoons orange liqueur*
> *2 tablespoons sugar*
> *½ teaspoon vanilla extract*
> *6 tablespoons heavy cream*
> *1 pint excellent ice cream—coffee, praline, or*
> *    butter pecan*
> *1 can Reddi-Whip*
> *1-2 tablespoons Nestle's Quik*
> *1 maraschino cherry (no stem), patted com-*
> *    pletely dry*

Slide the crust out of the crummy store pan into a fancy pie plate, so it looks like you went to a lot of trouble. If you tell your dad your mom's finally going to cook something, you can probably get him to spring for an expensive one. If the crust breaks, it's no big deal. Just fit the pieces into the dish and the filling will hold them together.

Melt the chocolate and put it somewhere so far away that you don't suddenly regain consciousness with brown smears on your face and a vague memory of a little voice screaming, "Give me your tongue!"

If you have a rich father, you can use a food processor or an electric mixer for the chocolate mixture. I, a Bundy, use a blender. An old blender. Blend the egg, yolk, coffee, and liqueur together. Pour in the sugar, rev up the old Waring, and blend until it's as frothy as a crinoline petticoat. Add the vanilla and blend again. You're going to add the chocolate now, and you have to do it fast and hard or you may find yourself humiliated by unsightly lumps. Kick the blender to get it going one last time, then use the ever-handy rubber spatula to scrape the chocolate in. When it's as smooth as I am, set it aside.

You can use a mixer to whip the heavy cream if you have to, but if you've got the muscles, an eggbeater is just fine. It's ready when the cream that stands up when you remove the beater doesn't flop over. Pour half the chocolate mixture into the center of the cream, then use a spatula to bring the cream from the bottom of the bowl to the top and into the chocolate, rotating the bowl a little with each stroke, so the cream doesn't deflate. Stop folding when almost all the chocolate streaks are gone. Fold in the rest of the chocolate, stopping just as soon as it's an even, smooth, creamy brown that will drive women wild. Pour it into the pie shell. Chip away enough ice in the freezer to make a level area for the pie to sit in. Freeze it until it's firm, at least 3 hours.

Take the ice cream out of the freezer about an hour before the chocolate filling's set and hide it where no one will find it—behind Kelly's history book, for example—or *it's* history. At the end of the hour, pour the liquid part of the ice cream into the pie shell and use a wooden spoon to beat the rest of it until it's soft enough to spoon into the shell. Pat the top with the spoon, a spatula, or your tongue until it's even, and freeze the pie again until the ice cream's firm, at least 2 hours.

Now you're ready for the master touch. Spray your Reddi-Whip on top of the pie in concentric circles. As you move inward, make each circle slightly higher than the one before until you've created a graceful, well-endowed mound. If the mood strikes you, sprinkle with the Nestle's Quik. Top with a well-chosen cherry. Freeze yet again for another 2 hours or until the woman of your dreams shows up, whichever comes first. Unless you wish to look truly lame, don't try cutting the pie unless your knife is hot, if you know what I mean.

*Serves 8—or 1 tired but happy couple.*

# Guests:
# They're Heeere!

I love having company over. It makes Al so miserable. There's nothing like a herd of embittered, obese women shoveling in cake and spewing venom to make him realize how lucky he is when there's only one woman around the house hammering him into an early grave.

There are two kinds of company: the kind that comes over and brings food, and the kind that comes over and wants food. Naturally, the second kind never gets invited again. But even the most considerate guests can forget to bring *everything* you need, so it helps to know how to cook something, anything, no matter how awful it is.

But enough about food. There's plenty of that later on. Now let's talk about the most important part of any dinner party—drinks. For example, guests expect a premium beer, not the swill they drink at home. So once in your life you're going to have to buy the good stuff. But only once; after that, you can reuse the cans over and over again.

Your teenage daughter can make that "pfft" sound she does so well as she "opens" the Michelob cans you've filled with Old Milwaukee. No one will be looking at her mouth as she leans over to hand them their drink. But no matter how many drinks you serve, there's always someone who's going to ask where the food is. It's right here!

## ASSORTED CANAPES

There's nothing like finger food to liven up a dinner party. It lets your guests know you're not stuffy, you want them to have fun, and your carpet is such a wreck, who cares if they drop things on it?

Canapes don't have to be a luxury item—you know, like Al thinks deodorant is. Remember that hunk of mystery meat that's been haunting your refrigerator for weeks? Slap it onto little pieces of bread cut into cute shapes and suddenly you're Martha Stewart. So what if your guests feed it to the dog—at least they know you cared enough to make it look nice. And if they actually eat one and feel like throwing up, all the better. You didn't make enough food for dinner anyway.

Here are some canapes guests really like:

*Pickle Boats.* Cut a slit in the middle of the flat side of a dill pickle half. Cut a piece of salami to look like a sail and stick it into the slit. Decorate the sail with a corporate logo in cream cheese.

*The Enchanted Forest.* Anybody can stuff a celery stick with Wispride, but you can do better. Fill them, then stick two together, and stand them up so you have a tree. If you want to blow their shorts off, make an entire landscape. Sail Pickle Boats on a lake of dip surrounded with broccoli bushes and animal crackers. Put a cucumber alligator at the edge of the lake with one of the animal crackers in his mouth.

**Nitrite Delites.** If you're going all out, little gourmet sausages like Slim Jims and Smokies are just perfect for pigs-in-blankets made with refrigerator rolls. If Ed McMahon finally comes through, stick 30 of them into a head of cabbage with toothpicks and serve over a can of Sterno to keep them warm.

**Jell-O Sticks.** Make in a square pan and cut into thin rectangles. The more colors, the prettier the presentation.

**Pet Shop Fire Sale.** Cover toast with thin slices of cheese, use a cookie cutter to cut them into animals, men, or exact replicas of U.S. currency, then stick them under the broiler. You can also put cut-out cheese in the bathroom so your friends think you can afford guest soap.

**Preemie Sundaes.** Top tiny cake squares with ice cream, nuts and hot fudge sauce. Aren't they cute?

**Crudities.** What you'd expect.

And now my favorite.


## STUCK ON YOU'S

I like to think of this as my tribute to the King. There was nothing he liked more than a peanut butter, bacon, and banana sandwich. And I know in my heart he would have loved them on potato chips if I had only gotten there in time.

*4 slices bacon*
*1 medium-size banana, peeled, cut into 14*
*    slices*
*12 medium-size potato chips, as flat as possible*
*    Creamy peanut butter*

Fry the bacon until it's crisp. Drain well on paper towels. Eat the two end slices of the banana. Spread each chip carefully with a thin layer of peanut butter. Crumble about ⅓ of a slice of bacon on top of each one. You could spread the peanut butter on the bacon and crumble the chips on top, but Elvis wouldn't have liked it that way. Top each chip with a banana slice.

You can make these up to an hour in advance. If you're not serving them right away, sprinkle the banana slices with lemon juice so they won't turn brown.

*Makes 12.*

## EASY SPICED TEAS

Sometimes there's a recipe so good, you just have to name it after yourself. This isn't it, so I named it after Kelly. Seriously, though, I did. This recipe makes that cheap tea you bought taste like the pretentious stuff they drink on "thirtysomething." So keep a jar of this in the back of the refrigerator and ladle it out to snobs like Steve and Marcy who would puke if they knew what was really in it. It'll give you something else to laugh at behind their backs.

> *½ cup hot water*
> *¼ cup frozen lemonade concentrate*
> *1 tablespoon ground cinnamon*
> *1 teaspoon ground cloves*
> *1 cup Tang powder*
> *1½ cups sugar*

Pour the hot water into a wide-mouth jar and stir in the lemonade concentrate until it's dissolved. Stir in the spices, then the Tang and sugar. Close and store in the refrigerator. Make sure you shake the hell out of the jar every time before you use it—nobody likes tea you can chew. Stir 1 teaspoon into a cup of tea, 2 in a mug.

*Makes more than you'll use in a lifetime.*

## BITCH CAKE

Sometimes I forget to buy unimportant things like flour. So shoot me. After all, what can you really do with it? Your family sees flour on the shelf and the next thing you know they're all lined up expecting cookies or something.

Al calls this my Bitch Cake because I only make it when I have the girls over to bitch. At least I think that's why he calls it that. It's really sad, he's not very well read. You know how those church group cookbooks have Scripture Cakes, where all the ingredients are from the Bible? My inspiration comes from books people really read, like Jackie Collins's *The Bitch*. I think of it as *my* bible.

I love this recipe. You don't need flour—you use up old crumbs. And the best thing is that it's pretty awful the first day. So if you give your family a taste the day you bake it, they won't

steal it when your back is turned. How many times have you been embarrassed by unsightly teeth marks on a cake you've brought out for your guests? Twenty-four hours later—when it's perfect—it's all yours.

> *7 separated eggs*
> *¾ cup honey*
> *¼ cup brown sugar*
> *2 tablespoons orange liqueur*
> *1 cup coarsely ground nuts*
> *¾ cup cookie crumbs*

Turn the oven to 350 degrees. Grease the bottom of a 10″ x 3″ springform pan, but not the sides or the cake won't rise. Beat the yolks, honey, sugar, and liqueur until they're smooth. Stir in the nuts and crumbs. Beat the egg whites until they hold stiff peaks, then fold them in.

Pour the batter into the pan and bake about 45 minutes, until a skewer inserted into the middle comes out clean. Cool it in the pan, then cut around the sides with a knife. Remove the pan's sides, then gently push the cake off the pan bottom onto a serving plate. Top it with vanilla ice cream or whipped cream with just a little sugar in it. If it's for the girls, forget the forks—they will.

*Serves 8 people.*

## DISHWATER FISH

I knew the dishwasher was good for something.

> *3 tablespoons soy sauce*
> *3 tablespoons lemon or lime juice*
> *1½ teaspoons ground ginger*
> *2 tablespoons olive oil*

*1 tablespoon sugar*
*⅜ teaspoon white pepper*
*6 sprigs fresh dill (optional)*
*6 1"-thick salmon steaks (about ½ pound each)*

Mix together the soy sauce, fruit juice, ginger, oil, sugar, and pepper. Tear off 6 pieces of foil, fold them in half and lay them out on your counter. The doubled piece of foil has got to be big enough so you can put one piece of fish on top and bring up the sides to enclose it completely.

Brush the salmon with the soy marinade. Turn it over so the marinade side is resting on the foil. Brush the other side of the salmon with the marinade and lay a piece of dill on top. Pour the extra marinade on. Bring the foil up around the salmon, then roll the edges down together to seal it well.

Very carefully put the packets on the top shelf of the dishwasher, making sure you don't tear the foil. Run the dishwasher—with the drying heater on—for the cycle that runs 50–60 minutes. For me, Cascade cuts the fishy taste, but nobody else likes it. Oh, and take out the Jet-Dri—we left it in once and Bud's voice changed back. Serve immediately.

*Serves 6 people.*

## COW PIES

Al's always saying, "Why can't you cook great food like I had in the Army? Chipped beef, powdered eggs, deep-fried potato eyes, spaghetti and doughballs, stuff I can only dream about now." And then he invites his old Sergeant over for dinner and expects me to cook something that great! Men are so inconsiderate. At least they could give you more than a few weeks' notice. You know, time enough to pack your bags and hightail it to Honolulu?

But once again I came through for Al with a really classy dish. Unfortunately, I didn't have anything to put on it, so I made this. All kidding aside, I'm proud of this recipe. I may even enter it in the "Oh No, Not Kentucky Fried Fritters Again, Mom" Cook-off.

If you can't find Chunky Beef Soup in your market, Chunky Sirloin Burger is just as good. Remember: For occasions like these, go for the cans without the dents.

*2 packages Pepperidge Farm frozen puff pastry*
        *shells (12)*
*6 cans (10¾ ounces each) Campbell's Chunky*
        *Beef with Vegetables Soup*
*¼ cup whole milk ricotta cheese*

*To bake the pastry shells:*
Read the package. It's that cardboard thing with last year's date on it.

*To make the filling:*
About 5 minutes before the shells are done, pour the soup into a wide-mesh colander set over a large skillet. The meat and vegetables will stay in the colander while the soup ends up in the skillet. Pour the meat and vegetables into a saucepan and heat over low until they're hot. At the same time, put the soup skillet over a medium flame. Stir in the ricotta cheese and cook, stirring a lot, until hot and as thick as gravy.

*To assemble the dish:*
Take the pastry shells out of the oven and put two on each plate. Take off the tops and scoop out any uncooked dough with a small spoon. Save it for doughballs for Al's spaghetti. God, I'm considerate. Spoon the meat and vegetables into the pastry shells, then spoon the gravy over them. Replace the pastry shell tops and chow down.

*Serves 6 people.*

# MOTEL SALAD

You're probably wondering why this recipe appears in the chapter devoted to guests. That's because our local motel is the only place left that will take the Bundys as guests. I guess it's because there's nothing in the rooms for us to destroy. Or at least there wasn't 4 years ago, which was the last time Al took us anywhere . . . except for that trip to Florida where we spent a lovely weekend with an ax murderer.

This is a lot like the Bundy Trail Mix we make at home. Of course at home everyone's so hungry all the time, the pickings on the floor are pretty sparse. Grape seeds, mouse droppings, dog hairs, and the occasional Lucky Charm are as good as it gets.

The exciting thing about a real motel is there's so much to choose from in the vending machines. Here's why I'm known as the Julia Child of Machine Cuisine:

Cut up the apples, oranges, pears, and whatever other fruit is on the metal menu and toss them together in your complimentary shower cap. Suck the chocolate off some Raisinets and an Almond Joy bar, then add the raisins plus the almonds and coconut to the fruit. Sunflower seeds and peanuts are tasty additions if they're among the selections.

Stir a little mustard into some orange juice, lemonade, or 7-Up (1 packet per carton or can) to make a nice tangy dressing and pour it over your fruit salad. Top with crumbled potato chips or corn chips or pretzels for extra crunch. Serve with the little packets of crackers and cheese or peanut butter.

Sometimes Kelly makes me so proud. She really wanted to help out her mom so much, she even did her homework for the first time since Sex Ed last year. (We thought she meant Sex Education, too, but Sex Ed turned out to be some bozo named Ed Jablonski . . . but that's another story.)

First she borrowed a tape recorder from her boyfriend Cobra so she could describe the recipe. Then he spent three whole nights helping her write it down. I don't know when those poor kids slept. It turned out so well, Cobra let her keep the tape recorder as a reward. Boy, some guys don't know when they're being used.

## THREE MUSKETEERS CHEESECAKE AND BOOK REPORT

Kelly Bundy here. My Home Ecch teacher, Mr. Puck, gave us this really stupid assignment. We had to write up this recipe he invented to "complement that great literary work you girls are privileged to study with Mr. Gregory in English class." I asked him if I could just say it was a good book and a good pie, but he didn't like that. And Mr. Gregory is making us write a book report to go with the recipe. I hate it when teachers gang up on you, so I wrote them both together! I figure they'll read it together anyway. Come to think of it, they do a lot of things together.

I got Bud to tell me what the book was about . . . and all he wanted in exchange was the key to the girls' locker room. But I told him he better tell me the real story this time, or I'd write "For a good time call Bud Bundy" on the boys' room wall.

*The Three Musketeers* actually turned out to be a pretty cool story. It's about these three guys, Larry, Curly, and Annette, but they had to change their names because the evil Cardinal Mickey "the Mouse" is after them. Larry's called Aramis because he's always putting on aftershave, Curly's called Bathos because he needs one, and Annette's called Ortho, but I didn't understand why. (Something about a mattress, I guess.) They have another friend called D'Arlene who just kind of hangs around. Finally Annette, who knows a lot about cheesecake, throws one in Cardinal Mickey's face and it's so good he hires them as the royal bakers. And this was the cheesecake:

> *1 graham cracker pie crust*
> *2½ ounces bittersweet chocolate*
> *½ cup milk*
> *1 envelope unflavored gelatin*
> *3 large eggs*
> *¾ cup light brown sugar*
> *1 pound cream cheese at room temperature*
> *1 teaspoon vanilla extract*
> *1 tablespoon white sugar*
> *Tasteless vegetable oil*
> *15 chocolate-covered almonds, chopped up into*
> *little pieces*

Move the dial with all the numbers on the front of the oven to 350. You need two pieces of cardboard. One is as long as the pie pan is from side to side, and twice as high as the pan. The other one is just like the other one, except half as long. Fold the bigger pieces in half, so both halves are as long as the short piece. Put the cardboard in your pocket, so somebody can't steal them like you did.

Melt the chocolate in a real tiny saucepan on the stove over a flame that doesn't come up very high until there are no lumps in it. This is a trick, because you have to stir it to get the lumps out and Mr. Puck didn't tell me that. Pour it out of the saucepan and into a bowl. Scrape out every last drop no matter what it does to your nails.

Heat the milk in a saucepan over another small flame until it's about as warm as a baby's bottle. You can use the chocolate saucepan if you clean it first—yeah, right, and tomorrow I join the WACs. Turn the heat off under the pan, but leave it where it is. Tear off the end of the gelatin envelope with your teeth and pour the powder out all over the top of the milk. Take one of those metal things with the handle and all the wires, and stir the milk over and over again until the gelatin disappears. If it disappears, I don't understand why you have to use it, but Mr. Puck always gets in a snit when I ask questions like that.

Now comes the real hard part. Separate the egg yolks from the egg whites. You'll have to get somebody to show you how. It's much too gross to explain. So then you put the yolks in the milk and stir it with that wire thing until it's smooth. Now you have to switch to a spoon. I think Mr. Puck just likes to make us wash dishes because that's when we tie our hair back and look like little boys. Turn the heat back on, but only a little bit. Stir in the brown sugar and mash the lumps—there'll probably be a lot of them.

So now you stir and stir and stir and stir the milk until you're so tired you want to throw up. But you keep stirring or you'll get an F and have to take the class over again. The milk is ready when you lift out the spoon and there's a thin layer of light brown stuff on the back that doesn't drip back off. It can take ages . . . like 8 minutes or something. Take the pan off the heat and shove it to the back of your workspace.

Now, as if that wasn't enough, you get to beat the cream cheese until it's smooth. If you're really nice to Mr. Puck and let him borrow your clothes, he'll let you use the food processor. When the cream cheese is smooth, stir in the vanilla stuff. If you let him borrow your eye shadow, you get to drink some. No, not the eye shadow. Vanilla tastes weird, but, hey, it's alcohol. Now you stir the milk into the cream cheese and get it real smooth again.

Now, for a really big thrill, you get to use those big electric mixers, the kind that are so loud you can't hear your Walkman. Put the egg whites into a mixer bowl and turn the mixer on. When they look like cheap bubble bath, all foam and no suds, dump in the white sugar. Keep mixing until they look like snow—thick and white and kind of pretty—and they don't fall over when you pick some up with a spoon. Stir them into the cream cheese real carefully. It's O.K. if there are still some white parts. That's a lot better than having to use that mixer again.

Now you have to get a math geek to help you out. Look for somebody with glasses, zits, and a blouse with a top button and offer to get her a date with the boy of her dreams. Nobody says you have to go through with it. What do you care if she never talks to you again? Anyway, so get the geek to divide up the cream cheese into thirds. She'll have to figure out how to stir 1⅔ cups of it into another bowl, then stir in all but a little bit of the chopped up chocolate-covered nuts. Thank God you get to leave the third part where it is so you don't have to talk to the geek for a minute.

Remember the cardboard? Take it out of your pocket and brush it with lots of tasteless vegetable oil. I brought in a bottle with a picture of Nancy Reagan on it, but then Mr. Puck tells me he meant the kind you can't taste. Well, why didn't he say so in the first place? Anyway, get your geek to put the cardboard in the pie shell, so it looks like a TV dinner tray with 3 empty places all the same size. Spoon the plain batter into one section and the chocolate batter into another part. The one with the chopped nuts goes in the third, and then you sprinkle the rest of the nuts on top of that part. Now real, real carefully, pull out the cardboard pieces without messing up the batter. Put the pie in the refrigerator, but don't spill it on the frogs from the bio lab.

*Serves people.*

> *"Just put me in front of a hot stove on a summer day, four burners going, grease splattering into my face, mixing with all the sweat. . . Aw, who am I kidding? I don't do any of that stuff."*—Peg

# Holidays:
# Celebrate the Moments
# of Your Life

Bundys love holidays. It's the only time we can embarrass other people into having us over. Who cares what they're celebrating—for Bundys free food is Christmas, Thanksgiving, and Kielbasa Day at Wrigley Field all rolled into one.

The only problem is, the day will come when all the cars are parked on *your* lawn, whether you're ready for them or not. Naturally you want to feed everyone as cheaply and easily as possible . . . without actually doing any work or spending any money. Believe me, if I can turn this house into a party palace, you can use these tips to plan the biggest blowout since Luke married Laura.

Try to buy reusable items. For example, I buy plastic toothpicks because I can wipe them off and use them over and over again. So what if Al uses them to clean his toenails, who'll know?

Plan your party the day after your neighbors throw one. We always show up right on time so Al can sneeze on the most attractive food platters before inconsiderate guests spoil the arrangement. When the hostess sees Al has a cold, she insists he go right home to bed and take the platters with him.

For cheap excitement, nothing beats a theme party. But make sure your guests know you have a theme. Otherwise they'll think Al always wears a feather duster in his hair and answers every question with "gobble gobble" (well, that's a bad example). Besides, if you throw decorations all over the house, people won't notice the furniture . . . and your children . . . and your husband . . . and your whole, shoddy, tragic life.

There are different kinds of themes, so here are some examples.

Make everything—and I mean everything—one color. It's a great excuse to buy a new dress, but the rest needn't be expensive or difficult. Here's one of those great little touches you can achieve with no work: If your theme is "blue," your toilet bowl water already matches! (Of course at our house, the theme would have to be yellow.)

Color coordination is also great because you don't have to cook anything special. Just throw one kind of food coloring into *everything*. By the way, if you put a drop of food coloring on your hand at the market and complain to the manager that it leaked, you can get a box of four colors for free.

If putting food coloring in everything seems like too much work, serve white food—whitefish with mushroom cream sauce, mashed potatoes and turnips, with white cake topped with vanilla ice cream and whipped cream for dessert. This meal is great when you're having kids over, since they can't stain the furniture. Unfortunately, you also have to play records by some white singer, like Barry Manilow or Donny Osmond.

But don't limit yourself to color themes. Be imaginative. Go all out. Here's a list of suggestions on how to give any party that Peg Bundy touch.

Single-food themes:
  **"All Peanut-Butter Buffet"**
  **"All Fried Festival"**
  **"Dry Cereal Celebration"**

International nights:
>  **"The Bundys Go Hawaiian"** (All right, so it's not international. I never claimed to be a geography expert.)
>  **"The Bundys Go Norwegian"**
>  **"The Bundys Go Away"**—you got it—you don't even have to be there!

And my most successful theme ever: "Have A Nice Day Night"—every dish smiles up at you with its own special "happy face" decoration.

Here are some menus and recipes from a few memorable get-togethers. I hope your parties are as much fun.

## EASTER DINNER

### DEVILED EGGS

### COKE-BASTED HAM

### CHOW MEIN NOODLE COOKIES

Easter stands for hope . . . every year I hope the dead will come to life. But Al says that the Lord knew enough to stay away from sex, and so does he. This year Al said all married men had to give up sex for Lent, and then he told me that so many women began going to church to pray for sex that the Pope extended Lent indefinitely. I asked the priest if this was true, and he said yes. But then again, he's met our kids.

So I spent most of Easter in the mall with Al's credit cards buying, well, who cared as long as it was expensive. The kids had a good Easter, too. We got them baby chicks, and they were delicious.

It's nice to serve a traditional Easter dinner, even if it does remind you that you have a family. And it's really nice when the whole family pitches in to help.

## DEVILED EGGS

Kids love Easter egg hunts, even when they're teenagers and too proud to admit it. You're probably asking who the hell wants to get up at 5 A.M. and crawl around outside in the damp grass hiding all those eggs? Get serious! Do you think you're the only people on the block with kids? Let me teach you how to stage an official Bundy egg hunt.

First, take a survey of the neighborhood—find out who the Christians are, who has lots of kids, who isn't very smart, who doesn't have a big dog. Chances are pretty good this will all be the same family.

Second, set your alarm for 5 A.M. on Easter morning and drag yourself to a window overlooking the chosen neighbor's house. Have the kids bring you coffee and a pair of binoculars.

Third, as the neighbors hide the eggs, map their location on a piece of paper.

Fourth, work quickly. As soon as the neighbors stumble back into the house, send your kids over to pick up the eggs. Don't be cruel—leave one or two.

Now you're ready to make your deviled eggs. It's a real attention-getter—and real Eastery—to make them in unusual colors, so I've included my favorites.

*6 hard-boiled eggs, peeled*
*2 heaping teaspoons mayonnaise*
*2 teaspoons prepared mustard*
*    Pinch of white pepper*
*1 tablespoon juice from any kind of sweet*
*    pickles*
*1 tablespoon prepared horseradish*

Halve the eggs lengthwise and scoop the yolks out into a bowl. Mash the yolks with a fork, then beat in the mayonnaise, mustard, pepper, pickle juice, and horseradish.

Here are the colors and flavors I like, but you can always improvise your own. I like to mix them, making a few in each color. Each color below is enough for 12 halves.

> *Pleasure Pink or Love That Red*—1 tablespoon cocktail sauce
> and red food coloring, OR
> use horseradish-beet mixture rather than just horseradish, OR
> *Golden Glow Yellow*—4 teaspoons French salad dressing and
> yellow food coloring, OR
> *Venetian Blue*—3 tablespoons canned chili with meat (no beans)
> and blue food coloring, OR
> *Misty Meadow Green*—3 tablespoons Parmesan cheese and
> green food coloring, OR

If you leave your cigarette on the edge of the bowl when you take an obscene phone call:

> *Obsidian Black*—ash of 1 cigarette (dig out filter) and black
> food coloring.

You can either spoon the yolk mixture back into the egg whites or you can put it in a pastry bag and pipe it out in a decorative pattern if you took the Advanced Egg Arts class at community college this year.

*Makes 12 halves.*

## COKE-BASTED HAM

Sometimes I just can't figure people out. I mean, what kind of idiot would send you a mail-order gift package of food that isn't already cooked? Someone from Al's family, of course.

After his Aunt Betsy got engaged to that rich Iranian, she had to get rid of all the pork in the house. She also had to get rid of all those tight leopardskin evening gowns and a case of Seagrams Golden Wine Coolers, but did she send me those? No, all I got was a lousy ham. Oh, I forgot—I've also got Al. I guess I'm the luckiest girl in the world.

*Half an uncooked ham with bone in (about*
*8 pounds)*
*1 onion, peeled and halved*
*2 cans Coke*
*2 tablespoons Scotch whiskey*
*1 teaspoon ground cloves*
*1½ tablespoons prepared mustard*

Turn the oven to 325 degrees. Put the ham in a shallow baking pan, fat side up. If it slides around, use the onion halves as wedges to hold it straight. If there's still a problem, cut a small slice off the bottom of the ham. And if that doesn't work, just tell the family it's already cooked.

Pour the Coke in around the ham and place it in the oven. Bake it 20 minutes per pound (about 2 hours and 40 minutes if it's 8 pounds), basting with the pan cola every 15 minutes.

Take the ham out of the oven. Cut off all the skin and all but a ⅛″ layer of the fat. Turn the oven to 400 degrees. Mix together the Scotch, cloves, mustard, and 2 tablespoons of the pan liquid. Leave the rest of the liquid where it is. Spread the mustard-clove mixture all over the ham.

Replace the ham (any side up) in the pan and put it back in the oven. Bake 20 minutes, then turn it over and bake 20 minutes more. Baste every 10 minutes during the entire 40 minute cycle. If the internal temperature hasn't reached 160 degrees, keep cooking or else the kids could get sick. Do you have any idea how expensive doctors are these days? And you wonder why people are Christian Scientists.

*Serves about 12 people.*

# CHOW MEIN NOODLE COOKIES

So these aren't exactly cookies. Calling them cookies makes it sound like for once you really cared enough to bake for your kids. Like you're Betsy Crocker or something. Sometimes a woman's got to do what a woman's got to do, and then again, sometimes she has to cook. So give it your all.

*10 ounces chocolate, milk, dark or mixed*
*¾ cup canned crispy chow mein noodles*
*¾ cup roughly chopped nuts, like walnuts or*
      *pecans*
*½ cup roughly chopped marshmallows*
*¾ cup butterscotch chips*

Melt the chocolate over very low heat and scrape it into a bowl. Stir in the noodles and nuts, then let it sit until the chocolate is cool but still liquid. Stir in the marshmallow and butterscotch chips—and anything else you've got—but don't mix it so much that the butterscotch melts. Drop soup spoonfuls onto wax paper on a baking sheet (you don't want to wash the baking sheet, do you?) and refrigerate. When they're cold, take them off the paper and throw them into a jar. Keep them refrigerated or they'll melt and all run together.

*Makes 60.*

# FOURTH OF JULY PICNIC

## MOLOTOV COCKTAILS
## POTATO CHIP CHICKEN
## FIRECRACKER CANNOLI

The Fourth of July isn't just about patriotism, Mom, and apple pie. No, it's also about sparklers, Roman candles, and big messy explosions. God I love the sight of those hunky paramedics as they haul off the bodies. It's better than television. So that's why this is a picnic menu. Who could stay inside on a wonderful day like this?

## MOLOTOV COCKTAILS

You've got a choice here. You can make these look fabulous or you can make a drink worth drinking. "Fabulous" is lighting up the night sky with a tray full of flaming cocktails. "Worth drinking" is not burning off all the alcohol. Style or substance— it's your choice. All I know is when I've gone to all the trouble of giving a party, I could use a good stiff one. And if I can't get that, I'll settle for a drink.

Don't flame these if you don't have heatproof glasses. Paper cups are definitely out. And if you want to be partygiver of the year, use ice cubes made of orange juice so the flavor isn't diluted when they melt.

> ½ cup sweet vermouth
> ½ cup Cointreau or Grand Marnier liqueur
> 1 cup vodka
> 2 orange slices, quartered
> Ground cinnamon

Mix together the vermouth, liqueur, and vodka, then pour into 8 heatproof wine glasses. Line the glasses up on a tray, light each drink, and have one of your kids (the one with the short hair) carry them out. When they've burned out, toss a couple of ice cubes in each one, and float a quartered orange slice with a sprinkle of cinnamon on top.

*Serves 8 people.*

# POTATO CHIP CHICKEN

Would you believe that there are really women who stand over a hot stove for hours cooking for their families? Don't laugh, it's true. I saw one on "Sally Jessy Raphael" last week, and God did she look old. It's all that heat that dries out the muscles that hold your breasts up.

As you may have guessed, my philosophy is to spend as little time in the kitchen as possible, kind of like Al's philosophy in the bedroom. Now if I could only get in and out of the kitchen as fast as . . . never mind . . . no use crying over spilt . . . So the whole point of this recipe is you bake it, but it tastes like fried. Have you noticed how many of these recipes involve lying to your family? Good, you're catching on.

*6 ounces thawed lemonade concentrate*
*1 cup Wishbone Italian Salad Dressing*
*2 tablespoons prepared mustard*
*1 teaspoon Worcestershire sauce*
*1 4-pound chicken, cut into serving pieces*
*2 tablespoons melted unsalted butter*
*2 cups crumbled potato chips*

Mix together the lemonade, salad dressing, mustard, and Worcestershire sauce in a large bowl. Add the chicken and turn the pieces to coat them in the marinade. Refrigerate 2–3 hours, turning the chicken once or twice if you feel like it, but why would you?

Turn the oven to 375 degrees. Pat the chicken with paper towels or aim a hair dryer at it to dry it really well. Throw out the marinade.

Put the butter in a shallow baking dish just large enough to hold the chicken in one layer and place it in the oven. When the butter's melted, take the dish out and put the chicken pieces in it. Turn them in the butter to coat them evenly. Pour on the chips and gently press them onto the chicken. Bake 1 hour until the chicken's cooked through. Serve hot or warm.

*Serves 4 people.*

## FIRECRACKER CANNOLI

The problem with this recipe is that you need cannoli tubes. Try buying those at the 7-Eleven! You've heard of creative cooks—now it's your turn. Just grab that hacksaw and go for the metal closet rod—as long as it's about 1" in diameter. Cut it into several 5½"–6" lengths. Come on, you've been nagging your husband for months because you want your closet customized.

So get rid of that ugly old rod (no, not your husband) and when he's lying back with his hand in his pants telling you how good dessert was, slip him that Closet Queens brochure.

> *1½ cups pre-sifted flour*
> *¼ cup brown sugar*
> *2 tablespoons sherry, Muscatel or other sweet*
> *    wine*
> *2 large eggs*
> *    Tasteless vegetable oil*
> *½ cup whole blueberries, fresh or frozen*
> *1½ cups strawberries, fresh or frozen, roughly*
> *    chopped*
> *1 recipe cannoli filling (next recipe)*
> *12 maraschino cherry stems*

Put the flour and sugar in a bowl and crumble them with your fingers until there are no more lumps. Push them to the sides so that you have a depression in the center (like the one in your life).

Beat the wine and egg together just enough to break up the yolks, then pour them into the center of the flour bowl. Mix the flour into the egg mixture with a fork, starting with the flour nearest the center, until everything's mixed together. Dump it out onto a board and throw it against the wall a couple of times to knead it until it's smooth. Check for roaches, then roll it into a ball, wrap it in Saran, and refrigerate it for at least 2 hours. It will keep in the refrigerator for 2 days.

Pour enough oil into a large skillet to come up about 2″ high. Dip the cannoli tubes in the oil, then put them aside. Heat the oil until it's about 350 degrees, so hot that when you drop in a small cube of bread it begins to sizzle in about a second. Cut the dough in half, rewrap one half, and stick it back in the refrigerator.

Cut the dough in 6 pieces. On a floured board with a floured rolling pin, roll one piece of dough into a rectangle 5½″ (or the length of your tube) x 4″ (wide enough to wrap around the tube with some overlap). Brush water on the inside of the edge that's going to overlap, then wrap the dough around the tube, and press the edges together to seal it very, very well. Gently roll the tube between your palms to smooth the dough out. Make as many cannolis as you have tubes for.

Put on an ovenproof mitt and carefully slide the cannolis into the hot oil. Fry, turning once if the top isn't browning, until brown all over. Remove with tongs or by sticking a wooden chopstick into each end, and drain on paper towels until it's cool enough to touch. Make sure you've drained the oil out of the center. Then, holding the tube with a potholder or tongs, push the cannoli off so you can reuse the tube. If it doesn't come off, hold the tube and twist the cannoli to loosen it.

Continue until all 12 cannoli shells are cooked, then let them sit until they're at room temperature. Unfilled shells can be stored at room temperature in a sealed container for up to 2 days.

Just before serving, stir the fruit into the cannoli filling without smashing it—unless you like the lovely brown color purple and red make when they're mixed. Spoon or pipe the filling into the shells. Stick a cherry stem into one end of each cannoli so that it looks like a firecracker.

*Makes 12.*

## CANNOLI FILLING

*2 pounds whole milk ricotta cheese*
*4 teaspoons vanilla extract*
*1 cup brown sugar, sifted if lumpy*

Beat everything together in a bowl until smooth. Press a sheet of Saran onto the top and refrigerate for up to 2 days.

## AL'S BIRTHDAY BASH

### MIDDLE AGE SPREAD
### BUNDY SPONGE CAKE

Another year, but not another dollar. In the marathon of life, Al hits the wall . . . again.

If you go to all the trouble of throwing your husband a big birthday party, then the least you can do is make sure he doesn't enjoy it. After all, you need to get something out of this too. And besides, if he has a good time he'll want one every year.

If he's happy some people actually showed up, tell him they came for the free food. If they bring presents, remind him he paid more than that for the bags of ice. And if he takes comfort in the fact that his life is half over, remind him that his body's so shot he'll never get anybody better-looking than you ever again.

If you really want to have a good time, make friends with expensive ingredients—like tiny shrimp—that your husband can't stand. (The symbolism alone is worth the expense.) And don't be ashamed to go for the obvious—he'll know what you're saying when you call the dip:

## MIDDLE AGE SPREAD

*½ pound cream cheese*
*3 cups cooked tiny shrimp (about 10 ounces)*
*½ cup sour cream*
*2½ tablespoons lemon juice*
*1½ teaspoons Worcestershire sauce*
*1 teaspoon ground nutmeg*
*Tabasco sauce, salt and pepper to taste*

Toss the cream cheese, shrimp, sour cream, lemon juice, Worcestershire sauce, and nutmeg into a blender. Sure you can use a food processor if you got yourself one for your husband's birthday. Run the machine until everything's mixed but you still have specks of solid shrimp. Add as much Tabasco, salt and pepper as you like.

*Makes 2½ cups.*

## <u>BUNDY SPONGE CAKE</u>

There are some people who think you actually have to go out and buy things like eggs, sugar, and flour. I bet they also think this is called sponge cake because it's spongy.

Here's the list of ingredients you need to sponge off your neighbors. If you're wearing curlers and Nair, you may even get them to deliver the stuff.

> *5 large eggs, separated, + 1 large white*
> *½ teaspoon almond extract*
> *1 teaspoon vanilla extract (don't let anyone*
>     *stick you with vanillin—insist on the real*
>     *stuff)*
> *¼ teaspoon salt*
> *½ teaspoon baking powder*
> *1½ teaspoons cream of tartar*
> *1¼ cups sifted cake flour or 1 cup + 2 table-*
>     *spoons regular flour*

Turn the oven to 350 degrees. Take a 10" round, 3" deep tube pan, preferably springform, and spray it with Pam. You can grease it instead unless you're out of Crisco. Don't forget to check the bedroom for a spare jar.

Beat the egg yolks until they're completely broken up. Beat in the almond and vanilla extracts, salt, and baking powder, then the sugar until the mixture's smooth.

Beat the egg whites until they hold soft peaks. Sprinkle the cream of tartar over them—you know, like I plan to sprinkle Al's ashes over the Caribbean when I take that trip on the insurance money— and beat until they hold stiff peaks.

Pour the yolk mixture into the center of the egg whites. Gently cut through the yolks with a spatula, then scoop up the whites from the bottom of the bowl, and fold them over the yolks. Continue to cut through the middle, turning the bowl ¼ turn each time, until there are no more white streaks. Fold the flour in the same way,

⅓ at a time. Don't mix too much or the whites will collapse like my life.

Pour the batter into the cake pan and bake about 50 minutes until a skewer inserted into the cake comes out clean. Put an upside-down plate on top of the pan. Wearing kitchen mitts, holding the pan and plate together, flip them over so the plate's on the bottom. Let them cool that way, then lift off the pan.

Light the candle, serve the cake, and (in my case) pry Al away from the nymphette who thought she'd heard Al say he puts on *shows* for a living. Then stand back, because when Al blows out a candle it's like being in the first car on the flume ride. It's really a shame that no one will eat wet cake, but you can eat it all by yourself the following day.

*Serves 8 people.*

# A VERY BUNDY CHRISTMAS

## CHRISTMAS TREE CENTERPIECE & DESSERT
## PIZZA DOMINOES
## MEATLOAF "CAKE" WITH MASHED POTATO "FROSTING"

## CHRISTMAS TREE CENTERPIECE & DESSERT

I was going to serve fruitcake—the one that's been in the family since Al's Uncle Righty got the good stuff out of Al Capone's vault just before Geraldo went in. But then Bud sold it to the museum as an ancient Egyptian hemorrhoid ring. So I created this work of art. Not bad for 90 seconds . . . unless, of course, you taste it.

> *1 newspaper*
> *Scotch tape*
> *Cream cheese, at room temperature, or white icing*
> *Trix cereal*

Roll the newspaper into a cone and tape it closed. Stand it on a small tray or a piece of plywood. Spread enough cream cheese on to make a layer as thick as the October *Cosmo*. Press the Trix—without crushing them—into the cheese to cover it up. Use the rest of the cheese to cover the tray—it will look like snow. Place it in the center of the table so everyone can enjoy it throughout the day.

## PIZZA DOMINOES

I don't know why people think the Bundys don't have that real holiday spirit. What could be more Christmasy than a red and green pizza? No, I don't mean a red pizza that's been around for a while—I'm talking about a salami pizza with some of that chopped up green stuff (you know, vegetables or herbs). And you don't even have to do much cooking.

Just slice your leftover pizza into rectangles the size of dominoes. Put two pieces together, sauce sides facing each other. Stick a wooden toothpick in to hold them together. Colored plastic toothpicks look really nice, but it's hard to pry them off your teeth after they've been fried.

Heat enough olive or Wesson oil in a large skillet to come up to the top of the dominoes. Heat over a high flame until the oil is just beginning to smoke. Put 4 or 5 dominoes in the hot oil, toothpick side up, and fry about 30 seconds until the tomato around the sides is browned and crispy. Use the toothpick to take them out of the oil. Drain them on paper towels while you fry the rest.

To make them look like dominoes, make dots with tubes of decorating icing or tomato paste. Arrange them in a pile that looks like it will fall apart if anyone takes one. No one will. More for you later. And for the next few weeks, every time Al takes a few seconds out of his busy schedule to play hide the sausage, he gets a tasty toothpick that he can suck on his way to work.

# MEATLOAF "CAKE" WITH MASHED POTATO "FROSTING"

It's Christmas, and you want to do a little special something for your family. But you've spent all your time shopping for yourself, there's almost no food in the refrigerator, and you've run out of credit at the deli. What can you do?

Here's a way to make the day just a bit more festive—a meatloaf that looks like a cake! It's a real flexible recipe. You don't have any breadcrumbs? Use cookie or graham cracker crumbs. No onions? Onion crackers instead of breadcrumbs. Out of celery and bell pepper? Who cares, nobody likes those anyway. No meat or potatoes? Give me a break, it's not *that* flexible.

For that really special touch, color the mashed potato topping to match the holiday. Since it's Christmas, use a little red coloring to make red and white candy-cane stripes. On St. Patrick's Day, try green; Halloween, orange; your anniversary, black.

A money-saving tip: There are some really great bargains on food coloring if you don't insist on FDA approval.

> *2 pounds regular ground beef*
> *½ cup crumbs*
> *2 large eggs*
> *½ cup finely chopped onion*
> *Just under a teaspoon ground mild chilies or paprika*
> *1 teaspoon salt + more to taste*
> *½ teaspoon white pepper + more to taste*
> *¼ cup + 3 tablespoons ketchup*
> *2 teaspoons Worcestershire sauce*
> *½ cup roughly chopped celery*
> *½ cup roughly chopped bell pepper*
> *3 cups ½" cubes of raw, peeled potato*
> *½ cup heavy cream*
> *6 tablespoons unsalted butter at room temperature*
> *Food coloring*

Turn the oven to 350 degrees. In a large bowl, squoosh the beef, crumbs, eggs, onion, chilies or paprika, 1 teaspoon salt, ½ teaspoon pepper, ¼ cup ketchup, the Worcestershire sauce, celery, and bell pepper together with your hands just until they're mixed. Scoop the mixture into a regular-size (about 8½″ x 4½″) loaf pan and pat into loaf shape.

Bake the loaf for 30 minutes. Drain off any liquid, then spread the 3 tablespoons of ketchup all over it. Bake 40 minutes more, draining off that brownish gook in the liquid in the bottom of the pan after about 20 minutes.

While the meatloaf is baking, boil the potato cubes just until you can stick a toothpick in easily. Drain them in a sieve, then mash in a bowl with the cream, butter, and as much salt and pepper as you want. Beat in the food coloring, 1 or 2 drops at a time, until it's the right color. Cover the bowl with foil and set aside.

Lift the meatloaf out of the pan with a long spatula and drain it on a paper towel. Put it on a serving plate and slide a 1″ wide strip of waxed paper under each of the meatloaf's 4 sides. At least half the strip should be showing. Spread the loaf with the mashed potato, then slide out the waxed paper strips. Remember, neatness counts (now if only Kelly could). Serve immediately.

*Serves 6 people.*

Boy, was I surprised when my neighbor Marcy insisted she help out with my new cookbook. I thought doing the dishes for the other 50 recipes would be a more appropriate gesture, but this is what I got instead.

## ANGEL WING CHIFFON CAKE WITH GOSSAMER PINK ICING

**by Ms. Marcy Rhoades**
Former Loan Manager
Kyoto National Bank
*Your Deposits Insured to $100,000 by the FSLIC*

I'd like to thank my dear friend Peggy for giving me the opportunity to contribute to this book. I must admit I was surprised when she told me she was putting together a Save the Sea Cows fund-raising cookbook. But I've always said there's a little bit of good in everyone . . . even Peggy. Isn't there?

My Angel Wing Chiffon is a beautiful, fluffy, tall, handsome cake. It exudes wholesomeness and proclaims a total reverence for life. I use oil instead of butter because it's much healthier and I strongly believe cows should not be kept in slavery to serve the whims of man- or womankind.

Eggs are fine, though—chickens don't have big brown eyes, so they obviously lack the sensitivity of higher mammals. I use unbleached flour—none of those nasty whiteners in our home. I also use brown eggs; they're more natural.

Unfortunately, sometimes we have to compromise our ideals. I made this recipe once with unrefined sugar and sea salt, but Steve's little face looked so disappointed when he tasted it that I resolved never, never to make him that unhappy again. Now I know cream of tartar is a chemical, but *you* try making a cake without it.

*2¼ cups unbleached pre-sifted flour*
*1½ cups C & H Pure Cane Sugar*
*3 teaspoons baking powder*
*¾ teaspoon salt*
*6 extra-large brown eggs*
*¾ cup Evian water*
*½ cup expensive vegetable oil*
*1½ teaspoons Madagascar vanilla extract*
*½ teaspoon crème de tartar (cream of tartar)*
*1 recipe icing (next recipe)*

Preheat the oven to 325 degrees. Strew a few small, luminous drops of oil in the bottom of a matched pair of 8″ x 3″ cake pans. Turn the pans upside down so their sturdy little bottoms show. Take a piece of wax paper about 16″ long and fold it in half so it's 8″ long. Then keep folding it in half along the same diagonal until it's just 1 or 2 inches across. Take the pleated triangle of paper and rest it on the cake pan so the point at the bottom of the long sides just tickles the pan's middle. Kindly but firmly restraining the paper with one hand, cut off any paper which extends past the edges. Unfold the paper and you should have a circle which nests snugly inside the pan. Put it in, giving it a secret little pat where it rests on the oil so it will stick. Repeat for the second cake pan. Then use a little more oil to lubricate the paper, but not the sides of the pan.

Now it's finally the time to let your ingredients know who's the boss. No more Ms. Nice Guy. Gently stir up the flour, the pure cane sugar (it helps to sing the C & H song here), baking powder, and salt until they're utterly mixed. Coyly tickle the egg yolks, water, oil, and vanilla together just until the yolks are broken up; leave them quivering, but desiring more. Stir them firmly into the flour mixture until the whole becomes moist and ready. And now, in yet a third bowl, begin to whip the egg whites and cream of tartar together. Whip them, beat them, excite them, until the peaks are stiff.

And now, your flour and egg white are finally ready to unite.

Fold them, roll them, mingle them together until they're one. Then, tear them asunder, forcing them into the 2 cake pans. Unite the pans in the warm and welcoming oven, where they will lie together for 50 minutes until a skewer, roughly thrust into the center, comes out hard and clean. If your oven temperature is uneven, switch positions halfway through. That's always fun.

Draw the cakes from their chamber of shared ecstasy, cooling their passions until they're no warmer than the sweet-scented air. But, sooner than you dared hope, the hunger that dares not speak its name glimmers and rages anew! In a sudden and irresistible assault, you seize a gleaming stainless steel blade and mercilessly slash around the outsides of the layers to sunder each from its pan.

With a plate on top of the pan, holding both in a firm but loving grip, tumble them over and over. The cake falls out innocently, helplessly onto the plate, entirely unprotected! Masterfully, you peel back the paper from the cake to expose its tempting nether regions, then cruelly turn it over again onto yet another plate. Not satisfied, you clutch at the other cake and do the same! If the cakes are plump and rounded on top, oh so slowly slice off the top of just one to make it flat.

While you and the cake are cooling one last time, catch your breath and make the icing. Ice the wounded layer first. Top with the intact layer, rounded side up, and then ice the entire cake. Light up a Lucky. It's been quite a nooner.

*Serves 5 couples, and they'll never know.*

## GOSSAMER PINK ICING

*1½ cups sugar*
*¾ cup Evian water*
*3 large egg whites*
*3 teaspoons Madagascar vanilla extract*
*¼ teaspoon cream of tartar*
*Pink food coloring (natural)*

Stir the sugar and water together in a medium-size Cuisinart saucepan over medium heat for about 30 seconds. Then, without stirring, let the mixture come to a boil and cook until it reaches 238–240 degrees on a candy thermometer. If you don't have a thermometer, jump in the Beamer and cruise by Williams-Sonoma; a kitchen without a candy thermometer is the kitchen of a complete loser. (Note to Peg: To test the temperature, dip a fork into the pan, and then plunge it into cold water. If there are long strings as you pull the fork out, it's ready.)

While the sugar is cooking, beat the egg whites until they've got lots of little bubbles on top. Add the vanilla and cream of tartar and beat until they hold stiff peaks and aren't glossy anymore. Set aside.

When the sugar mixture's ready, begin beating the whites again. Very slowly pour in the sugar mixture, beating constantly. Beat until all the sugar's added, the frosting is cool, and it holds rounded peaks when you lift out the mixer.

*"Hello? Pizza man?"—Peg*

# The 6-Minute Gourmet

Unlike the morons who live by the "60-Minute Gourmet," I can't be expected to spend all my time in the kitchen. If you can't do it in under 6 minutes, it's not worth doing. Unfortunately, Al thinks that rule applies to everything.

The recipes in this chapter are super-fast. Sure, there's that special occasion stuff in the previous chapters, but this is real life here. Learn how to plan your time. Never do anything that looks hard unless and until there's somebody watching.

You can learn to serve food quickly, too, especially if you use the container you cooked it in. Just put the skillet right on the table, on top of a library book so you won't damage the formica. If you've got company, announce, "Attencion! ees very, very hot!" in a bad French accent. Tell people it keeps the food hot and that French gourmets do it all the time (God, was I surprised to find out that was true). The trouble is, Al doesn't believe me anymore when I tell him that the French do things a certain way; he still runs out screaming whenever I mention the Folies Bergere suite of Ralph's Moulin Rouge Adult Motel in Gary.

# REMOTE CONTROL MERINGUES

This recipe is the epitome of what this chapter is all about—cooking while you sleep. Sometimes I'm so good I scare myself. I know I scare Al, but that's not as hard as it used to be. Unfortunately, neither is Al.

You can bake these as cookies, or you can make little shells for ice cream and stuff if you're the kind of person who cares what color toilet paper goes in what bathroom or empties the ashtrays every week even if they're only half full. Since this is only a book, let's pretend and do shells.

*4 large egg whites*
*½ teaspoon cream of tartar*
*2 teaspoons vanilla extract*
*1¼ cups confectioners' sugar*
*¼ cup crushed Heath bars*

Turn the oven to 400 degrees. Cover two baking sheets with two pieces of a brown paper bag. You can actually go out and buy something called cooking parchment, but why drag yourself to the market to buy something you already have lining the garbage can.

Draw six 6″ circles on each piece of paper. Mix together the egg whites, cream of tartar, and vanilla and beat the hell out of them until there's lots of foam. Beat some more as you stir in the sugar. Beat until you get firm pointy white peaks—like the ones that would have made me Miss Chicago Bares for 1975 if Al hadn't managed to chew his way out of those restraints. Then, real gently, so you don't collapse the meringue the way Al did my dreams, stir in the candy.

Spoon the meringue onto the 12 circles. Use the back of the spoon to spread each circle out so it's shallow in the middle with a wall around the edges. Put them in the oven, turn off the heat, padlock the oven door and go to bed. Take them out in the morning, or 4 hours later if there's an Arnold Schwarzenegger film festival on Movies Till Dawn.

*Makes 12 shells.*

# ALL PURPOSE APPLE SLUDGE

I invented this recipe the day Kelly crashed a borrowed convertible into an apple tree, and all those apples fell into the front seat. We would have offered to pay for the damage, but Kelly was only 13, and besides, she didn't know whose car it was. The poor girl was so traumatized she swore she'd never get into the front seat of a car again.

So I had all these damaged apples and I thought, hey, it doesn't hurt to be a mom once in a while. I made Brown Betty, applesauce, baked apples, and apples marinara, until I couldn't stand the sight of them. But there were all these pathetic apples left, their tiny stems frantically waving at me.

Exhausted, overwhelmed, my mind reeling, I finally remembered what I had forgotten—APPLE PIE! When I was a kid growing up in America, my family, like so many others in the '50s, lost touch with the land. When they wanted a pie, they reached for the Ritz. I was twenty-five before I found out you could make apple pie out of apples. Go figure.

If you always keep some Sludge in the house, you can make A Good Hot Lunch (page 10), Yellow Snow (next recipe), or a Mock Ritz Cracker Pie with very little work. By the way, if you make a really bad pie crust, no one will eat it and you can re-use the same one again and again.

You can also serve Sludge plain, or on top of pound cake or shortcake with whipped cream. Here's how:

*¾ cup unsalted butter, chopped into small pieces*
*12 cups tightly packed, peeled, thinly sliced apples*
*¼ teaspoon ground ginger*
*¼ teaspoon ground cinnamon*
*¼ teaspoon ground nutmeg*
*¾ teaspoon curry powder*
*¾ cup white sugar*
*¾ cup brown sugar*
*¾ cup white wine*

Melt the butter in a large pot over medium-low heat. Add the apples and stir them now and then until they've absorbed all the butter. While they're cooking, mix together the spices, curry powder, and both sugars, rubbing them between your fingers to get out any lumps.

Stir the spice mixture into the pot. Pour in the wine and bring to a boil over high heat. Turn the heat to low and simmer until the apples are tender and there's a thick syrup in the pan. Spoon into wide-mouth jars and refrigerate up to a month. Serve hot, warm, at room temperature, or cold—I won't be there to eat it.

*Makes enough for 1 pie.*

## YELLOW SNOW

Al says this is where the expression "Don't eat yellow snow" came from, but I know he's just kidding. Of course I also thought he was kidding when he said he'd taken that job at the shoe store. So one day I gave him real yellow snow to teach him a lesson—and he asked for more. That's my Al, the original budget gourmet.

This is a good diet dessert because the egg whites and gelatin make a little go a long way. If your teeth are in the shop, you can use pureed Apple Sludge or applesauce instead of apple slices.

*¼ cup hot water*
*1 tablespoon unflavored gelatin*
*1½ cups cold or room temperature Apple Sludge*
*(previous recipe), canned apple pie filling*
*or spiced applesauce*
*6 tablespoons sugar*
*2 large egg whites*
*4 teaspoons cookie crumbs, like macaroons or*
*gingersnaps (optional)*

Put the hot water in a bowl with high sides. Sprinkle the gelatin over it and let it sit 1 minute to dissolve just a bit. Then stir until smooth.

Stir in the apples or applesauce, squeezing the apples through your fingers if you want to break them up a bit. Beat in the sugar. Beat the egg whites until stiff, then fold them in. Spoon into 4 beer mugs—or parfait glasses if your dead aunt stuck you with her Au-sable Chasm collectibles—and chill in the refrigerator. Sprinkle the tops with the crumbs just before serving.

*Serves 4 people.*


# STRAWBERRY PINA COLADA ICES

Tell your husband you've brought him something fast, fun, and alcoholic. Then watch him sink back into despair when he realizes it's not The Amazing Andrea from Club Med.

>    *2 16-ounce boxes frozen strawberries (whole or*
>        *sliced) in syrup, thawed*
>    *5 tablespoons dark dry Bacardi Rum*
>    *5 tablespoons Cointreau or Grand Marnier*
>    *¼ cup Bacardi Pina Colada Concentrate*

Puree everything but half a box of berries in a food processor or blender. Stir in the rest of the berries, pour into a plastic container and freeze. Scoop onto plates, alongside fruit salad, or on top of Remote Control Meringue shells.

*Serves 10 people.*

# PAN-GRILLED BEEF

Almost everything in this recipe comes from Chinese and Mexican take-out places. Except, of course, the expensive stuff—the beef and the fruit juice. Well, I guess only a couple of things come from take-out joints, but it's a good recipe anyway. Why shouldn't it be? Chinese food is great because it cooks fast. Mexican food is great because it's already made.

> *¼ cup orange juice*
> *¼ cup lemon juice*
> *3 Chinese restaurant packets soy sauce*
> *¼ cup sesame oil*
> *1½ pounds flank steak, frozen*
> *Vegetable oil if necessary*
> *8 corn tortillas*
> *Chunky salsa poured into a large strainer*
> *to get rid of the icky liquid*

Mix together the fruit juices, soy sauce, and sesame oil in a bowl. Cut the fat off the steak and refrigerate it for later. Cut whatever steak is left into very thin slices and stir it into the bowl. Cover it with Saran Wrap and refrigerate it 6–12 hours.

Heat a medium-size cast-iron skillet until it's really hot. Add half the beef fat and stir it around so that some of it melts. Push the unmelted fat to the side of the pan and add half the beef. If it sticks to the pan, you should have added a tablespoon of vegetable oil, but it's probably too late now. What the hell, try it anyway.

Cook the beef, flipping it once, until there's no more red and it has some ugly dark patches. Take it out of the pan with a slotted spoon. Cook the rest of the beef in the rest of the fat the same way. Give your husband the fat—if he tastes meat, the excitement could kill him. Come to think of it, give him the meat. All of it.

*Serves 4 people.*

# PINEAPPLE RIGHTSIDE-UP CAKE

Why spend all the time it takes to make an upside-down cake when you can *buy* a perfectly good cake and fake it? Beats me.

*¼ cup unsalted butter cut into small pieces*
*½ cup dark brown sugar*
*1½ tablespoons heavy cream*
*3 slices canned pineapple*
*12 ounce loaf of pound cake*

Put the butter and sugar in a small skillet. Turn the heat to low and stir until the sugar's completely dissolved. Stir in the cream. Take the pan off the heat and hide it so you don't keep tasting the caramel.

Slice the rounded top off the cake so it's flat. Cut the pineapple slices in half and pat them dry. Set the cake on a foil-covered baking sheet. Turn the broiler on.

Arrange the pineapple slices along the top of the cake so they look like this: (((((. It's also okay if they look like this: ))))). Spread the caramel over the top and sides of the cake and pineapple with a small spatula. Put the baking sheet in the oven so the broiling element is 1 or 2 inches above the top of the cake. Broil 2–3 minutes until the sugar is bubbling. Watch carefully so it doesn't burn.

Take the cake out of the oven. If any of the caramel slid off the cake and onto the foil, just slap it back on with the spatula. Bring the cake out to the table so everyone can see how great it looks. Then take it back in the kitchen and serve pineapple Lifesavers for dessert. Arrange them on a platter so they look like this: OOOOOO.

*Serves 6 people if you're out of Lifesavers.*

# CHICKEN WHICH MAKES ITS OWN GRAVY

I got this recipe from Mom, who got it off an old evaporated milk package. All I know is, it was love at first sight. Why should you do all the work? Let your food lend a hand, or a wing in this case. And these days with everything imported from Korea or somewhere, it's nice to know your gravy was made in the good old USA.

This really brings back memories. Mom used to make enough for the whole family, and then we'd all sit in the kitchen and watch her eat it. I always wondered how it tasted, but Mom said, "Keep that gorgeous figure until you land that nice Hefner boy." But I had bigger plans. I wonder what they were.

Maybe I'll pass the recipe on to my little girl when she grows up . . . if she can read by then.

*2 tablespoons vegetable oil*
*2 tablespoons unsalted butter, roughly chopped*
*1 chicken, 3½–4 pounds, cut into serving pieces*
*6 tablespoons flour mixed with ¼ teaspoon*
    *pepper*
*1 cup finely chopped onion*
*¼ pound fresh mushrooms, roughly chopped*
*2 celery stalks, roughly chopped*
*⅔ cup evaporated milk*
    *10½-ounce can Campbell's condensed Cream*
        *of Mushroom or Cream of Celery Soup*
*¼ cup grated Parmesan cheese*
*⅛ teaspoon paprika*
*½ teaspoon prepared horseradish*

Turn the oven to 425 degrees. Stir the oil and butter together in a large ovenproof pot like a Dutch oven, and place it in the oven until the butter's melted. Roll the chicken pieces in the seasoned flour.

Take the pot out of the oven and stir the oil and butter until mixed. Cram the chicken pieces in, skin side down, in one layer. Sprinkle on any flour that didn't stick to the chicken. Bake, uncovered, for 30 minutes.

Take the chicken pieces out of the pot and put in the onion, mushrooms, and celery. Put the chicken back in, skin side up. While it's cooking, mix together the milk, soup (without any water added), cheese, paprika, and horseradish.

Turn the heat down to 325 degrees. Pour the milk mixture over the chicken, then turn the chicken pieces over. Cover and bake 15 minutes more until you've got a thick gravy.

*Serves 6 people.*

# WATER FONDUE

Not only do your guests do their own cooking, you also get tomorrow's lunch out of it. Make sure you give your guests chopsticks so they lose lots of stuff in the pot. Not just food, maybe even rings and watches.

Save the flavor packet that comes with the ramen noodles. Sprinkle it on popcorn when you don't have time for dinner before the movies.

> *6 tablespoons sake, sweet rice wine or sherry*
> *2" slice fresh ginger, smashed then minced*
> *½ cup soy sauce*
> *1 garlic clove, smashed then minced*
> *2 pounds raw lean beef, sliced very thin*
> *4 cups bean sprouts*
> *6 cups greens, like spinach, torn into bite-size*
> *    pieces*
> *8 stalks celery, thinly sliced*
> *8 small carrots, thinly sliced*
> *1 package beef-flavor ramen noodles*

Mix together the sake, ginger, soy sauce, garlic, and beef in a bowl, cover with Saran and marinate in the refrigerator 2–24 hours.

Put an electric wok, skillet, or large fondue pot on the dining table. Fill it halfway up with cold water. Take the beef out of the marinade and arrange it on a large platter with the bean sprouts, spinach, celery, and carrots, each ingredient in a separate pile. Cover the platter with Saran and place it in the refrigerator, along with the beef marinade.

Since you're serving steak, fill your guests up with cheap stuff before dinner. When you run out of pork rinds, pour the marinade into the wok. Turn the wok on high and bring the platter out to the table. When the liquid comes to a boil, turn the heat down so it just simmers. Set everyone loose with chopsticks or fondue forks. If they can't figure out that they're supposed to cook their food over the wok, let them starve.

When everyone's done, or before if you're fast enough, scrape the remaining food into the pot and bring it into the kitchen. Reheat it the next day, stir in the ramen noodles, and cook until they're done. Chew thoroughly, jewelry has a tendency to crunch.

*Serves 8 people.*

## ICE CREAM DICE

If you can only find regular size chocolate chips, make really big dice. For a handy commuter snack, roll a pair of these in pink coconut shreds and hang them on your rear view mirror with a black licorice whip. Eat fast.

*Brick of vanilla ice cream*
*Miniature chocolate morsels*

Use a knife dipped in warm water to cut the ice cream into 1½″ cubes. Put the cubes in the freezer until they're very cold. Then stick 1 to 6 morsels in each side, so they look like dice.

Serve in a plastic cup, but don't let your friends roll them on the rug.

This is from Marcy's husband, Steve who says he's a millionaire in training. Is that what they call bank tellers these days? Anyway, here's his contribution. I can't believe we worked so hard on his peas and carrots. Hasn't he ever heard of Birds Eye? But please, don't say anything. Steve and Marcy are the only friends we've got.

## SALADE DE PETITS POIS STEVEN RHOADES AVEC SAUCE MAYONNAISE AU FROMAGE ET MOUTARDE

I'm a reasonable man. I know others don't feel as strongly as Marcy and I do about animal rights. However, in the interest of mutual tolerance of diverse viewpoints, I've included the instructions you'll need in the event you've made the morally debatable decision to eat . . . dare I say it . . . meat. I am, of course, only guessing at the exact amount of Farmer John's thick sliced bacon you'll need for this dish and the way in which one cooks it.

Marcy and I share many of the household chores and I do a great deal of the cooking. I try to prepare dinner before she gets home. I hate for her adorable and extremely sensitive little nose to be assailed by those nasty cooking odors, and for her cute and lovely eyes to be irritated by fumes.

This is, by the way, a very elegant recipe, one which I've been proud to serve to company time and time again. Being an investment banker and tied to the world economy, I am, of course, much more accustomed to dealing in metric measurements. But I've included the closest U.S. equivalents since I don't believe anyone, even Peg, should be denied access to true gastronomic excellence, no matter how limited his or her education.

*405 freshly shelled petits pois (approx. 250 ml,*
*or 1 cup)*

*3 baby carrots (10 grams, or ⅓ ounce, each),*
*cut into 140 matchsticks 1.5 mm x 1.5*
*mm x 2.5 cm (¹/₁₆″ x ¹/₁₆″ x 1″) in size*
*(total of 125 ml, or ½ cup)*

*1 scallion (1 cm, or ⅜″, wide at the base),*
*white and light green section only (9 cm,*
*or 3⅜″, long)*

*30 grams (1 ounce) baby spinach leaves (250*
*ml, or 1 cup, tightly packed but without*
*bruising)*

*2 25-gram (⅞-ounce) 3 mm x 2.5 cm x 20 cm*
*(⅛″ x 1″ x 8″) slices smoked bacon, cut*
*into a total of 16 pieces, each 2.5 cm (1″)*
*long—but I'm only guessing on these*
*measurements*

*20 or 25 ml (4 or 5 teaspoons) extra virgin*
*olive oil*

*1 large white mushroom (35 grams, or 1.2*
*ounces), cut into 5 mm (³/₁₆″) cubes (total*
*of 100 ml, or 6⅔ tablespoons)*

*1 recipe Sauce Mayonnaise au Fromage et*
*Moutarde (next recipe)*

*10 ml (2 teaspoons) raspberry or balsamic*
*vinegar*

*0.6 ml (⅛ teaspoon) freshly ground pepper*

*12 ml (2½ teaspoons) fresh basil, cut into*
*shreds 1.5 mm (¹/₁₆″) wide x 2.5 cm (1″)*
*long*

*11 ml (2¼ teaspoons) fresh mint—spearmint,*
*apple, or Corsican, cut as the basil*

Fill the bottom half of a steamer pot with 5 cm (2″) of water. Bring it to a boil over low heat. Put the peas in the top section and place in the pot. Cover and cook until the peas are *al dente.* The only way to ascertain this with petits pois is to taste one every 50 seconds—that's what the extra 5 peas are for.

Pour the contents of the pot into a 1.5-mm ($\frac{1}{16}''$) gauge stainless-steel-mesh strainer with a diameter of 13 cm (5″) and shake gently to drain thoroughly. Remove 25% of the peas and spread them on a paper towel. Using your palm, gently roll the peas on the towel until all sides are dry. Pour the peas into a bowl with a bottom diameter of 20 cm ($7\frac{7}{8}''$). Repeat with the rest of the peas in 3 more batches. Fold the carrots into the bowl without crushing the peas. Set the bowl aside. Cut the scallions into slices 2.5 mm ($\frac{1}{8}''$) thick and separate the rings. Set them aside.

Wash the spinach leaves very well, then pat dry very carefully. Tear them by hand into pieces 2.5 cm x 5 cm (1″ x 2″) if larger than that. Arrange them on two 28-cm (11″) dinner plates as follows: leaving a 4-cm ($1\frac{1}{2}''$) border and a 10-cm (4″) diameter circle in the center uncovered, strew the spinach around each plate to form a 5-cm (2″) ring. It should resemble a wreath of laurel leaves. Set the plates aside.

Place the bacon pieces, not touching each other, in a copper skillet with a 15–18 cm ($5\frac{7}{8}''$–$7\frac{1}{16}''$) diameter base. Turn the heat to medium and let it cook 1 minute 55 seconds. Turn the pieces with tongs and cook 1 minute 5 seconds more until the edges are browned and most of the interior fat is golden brown. Take them out with a slotted spoon and drain well on a paper towel. Again, I'm only guessing on the meat directions.

Turn the heat down to low and add 10 ml (2 teaspoons) of the olive oil. If you didn't use the bacon, pour 15 ml (3 teaspoons) of the oil into the skillet. In either case, heat the oil until it's 140 degrees C (285 degrees F), too hot to hold your hand 5 cm (2″) above the skillet for more than 2.6 seconds.

Immediately add the scallion and mushroom to the skillet. Cook a total of 5 minutes and 40 seconds, stirring briefly every 70 seconds. They're done when the mushroom pieces are $\frac{9}{16}$ their original size and lightly browned all over. Using a slotted spoon, transfer the scallion and mushroom to the bowl of peas and toss gently.

Using your 2.5-cm (1″) rubber spatula, fold the mayonnaise dressing into the peas. Divide the pea salad into halves of 105 ml (7 tablespoons) each. Now, if you insist, fold the bacon into half of the salad. If, however, you have any respect for others' sensibilities, place it on the open circle in the center of your dinner plate, so it will be completely hidden under the peas. Spoon on the pea salad, then prod it into a smooth mound.

Sprinkle each spinach circle with 0.3 ml (1/16 teaspoon) pepper and 5 ml (1 teaspoon) each olive oil and vinegar. Sprinkle both the spinach and peas with the basil and mint. Serve immediately.

*Serves 2.0 gastronomes.*

## SAUCE MAYONNAISE AU FROMAGE ET MOUTARDE

*30 ml (2 tablespoons) mayonnaise from your
     favorite recipe
6 ml (1¼ teaspoons) freshly grated aged
     Parmigiano-Reggiano
5 ml (1 teaspoon) Maille moutarde de Dijon
     au vin blanc
5 ml (1 teaspoon) freshly squeezed lemon juice
4 ml (¾ teaspoon) freshly squeezed pink
     grapefruit juice
1 ml (¼ teaspoon) freshly grated nutmeg*

Spoon the mayonnaise into a bowl with a bottom diameter of 6.5 cm (2½"). Using a 2.5-cm (1") wide rubber spatula, lightly beat in the cheese, mustard, and nutmeg. Beat in the lemon and grapefruit juice. Cover the bowl with a good grade of plastic wrap (about 13 microns, or 1/2000", thick) and refrigerate until you're ready to use it.

*Makes 50 ml (3⅓ tablespoons).*

# Restaurant Favorites:
# Free At Last, Free At Last!

On the one hand, going to a restaurant is good. You get to eat real food that you don't have to cook. On the other hand, it's bad. Your family will find out certain unpleasant truths, like milk shouldn't plop when you pour it.

But before you go out to a restaurant, you should learn how to behave. It's considered impolite to slip a waiter your phone number if you see him holding hands with another waiter in the back of the room. Don't laugh at other diners, especially the fat woman who orders a chocolate shake and the diet plate.

Never, ever take imprinted matches or sugar from a restaurant. The restaurant doesn't care, but it's a sure tip-off you've been somewhere that even *your* family can't miss. Oh, and introduce the silverware you steal gradually, so your neighbors won't notice. Or, better still, hide it until you have settings for 8, then announce it was left to you by a distant relative.

Unfortunately, there are times when you don't have enough money, and you have to take your husband along to pick up the check. He may insist on bringing the kids, but, hell, he probably still thinks they're his. My mother always said, "Never pick up a check or a shoe salesman, but if you have to choose one or the other, take the salesman." Thanks a lot, Mom.

But 2 years ago, something happened that took the joy out of restaurant-going for all the Bundys. *Our* home away from home, that true symbol of America, the great burger joint Johnny B. Goode's, shut its doors forever. God, that hurt. It's where I met the man I wanted to spend the rest of my life with. I met Al there, too.

People used to flock there to see the grease spot on the wall where Al rested his head. I fell in love with him the first year he won the Chug-a-Spud contest. I can still see him now, hands tied behind his back, face on the table, nostrils flaring, struggling for breath as he annihilated those bags of fries, paper and all. I can still see the younger, unbeaten-down-by-life me, leading the cheers. It's the most excited Al's ever made me, but how was I to know that then? Well, you can't tell everything about a man by the size of his tongue.

Johnny B. Goode's, though, lives on in our hearts, in Al's cardio-vascular system, and on our table. Somehow, on that closing night, Kelly convinced old Spike, the owner, to let her have his secret recipes. Al was so proud of her he let her keep the twenties she found in the cash register. Spike had a heart attack and died that night—happy, Kelly says—but if he had lived, I know he would have wanted us to cash in on those recipes. I know I do. Here is the Bundy favorite.

## "SIXTEEN TONS" CHEESEBURGER

Spike always said this was the burger you had to eat with a pick. It was an authentic #9 coal fire that gave it that tasty all-carbon crust. Unfortunately the energy crisis of the early '70s sent coal prices through the roof. Spike held out for a while but then the EPA coal-smoke crackdown was too much for him. After the heart attack, he finally gave up and switched to a mustard glaze.

We all got on his case about turning the place into a fern bar, but his burger was still pretty macho stuff. If you have any coal lying around the house, though, go for it.

*1 pound lean ground beef*
    *Pepper to taste*
*½ teaspoon ground cumin*
*2 teaspoons cider vinegar*
*2 slices Swiss cheese, chopped into small pieces*
*2 tablespoons mild cheddar, chopped or crum-*
        *bled into little pieces*
*1 tablespoon blue cheese, crumbled*
*1 tablespoon prepared mustard*
*2 tablespoons plum or apricot jelly, jam or*
        *preserves*
    *Warm garlic bread*
    *Crisp iceberg lettuce*
    *Sliced tomatoes*

Flatten the beef into two 6″ circles. Sprinkle each with pepper and half the cumin and vinegar. Put half the cheese in the center of each, leaving a 1″ border of beef uncovered. Bring up the sides of each burger and press it closed to seal the filling in.

Mix together both mustards and the fruit stuff. Brush the burgers with it, then barbecue or broil 'em, basting with the remaining mustard mixture until until you've used it all. Turn the burgers once. When they're browned, serve them on the garlic bread with the lettuce and tomatoes.

*Serves 2 people.*

## "AIN'T THAT A SHAKE"

Spike discovered this recipe when he blacked out in the middle of making one of his, to be truthful, pretty average milkshakes. Must have been his first stroke. He was just looking over into the Hamilton Beach and the next thing we knew there was Brylcreem, broken dentures, and bloody gobs of hair flying around the room. The place was a mess.

Al decided to help out by cleaning up, but when he got to the malt machine there was a sudden hush in the room. As far as we could tell, some of those Red Hots Spike was always chewing and the tufts of his hair which were caught in the rotor had combined to make milkshake magic. No matter how much we begged, Spike said we had to find a substitute for his hair—there just wasn't enough to go around. So we used pudding mix instead.

So here's Spike's special milkshake. You've got to follow the recipe exactly. Once, when I was out of Red Hots and Tic Tacs, I tried Big Red. It was a disaster. Maybe that stuff on the bottom of my shoe wasn't gum after all.

*1 cup cold milk*
*6 Red Hots or 12 cinnamon Tic Tacs*
*5 tablespoons Jell-O Chocolate Pudding Mix*
    *powder*
*2 ice cubes*
*1 large scoop ice cream*

Put the milk, Red Hots, pudding mix, and ice cubes in a blender and blend until you can't hear the candy rattling around anymore. Add the ice cream and blend until thick and frothy. Serve at once.

*Makes 1 shake.*

# "DEVIL OR ANGEL" CAKE

After his first serious head injury of 1974, Spike developed a split personality for several months. It was kind of sad to watch. He'd be making a cake, and one hand would be trying to add the chocolate, while the other was pushing it away. "No, no, no. Yes, yes, yes. Chocolate! Butterscotch! Did you remember to feed the cat? Why is it always my job?"

It got to the point where he'd come to the diner, then show up again without having left. His personalities were multiplying so fast that he had to let all the help go because no one else could get behind the counter. We would have been crazy with worry, but he had us beat there too. Something had to be done, but, hey, it wasn't our problem. Besides, it's a hell of a cake.

> *1 cup unsalted butter*
> *4 ounces unsweetened chocolate*
> *1 cup white sugar*
> *1 teaspoon baking powder*
> *1¼ teaspoons vanilla extract*
> *4 large eggs*
> *2 cups pre-sifted flour*
> *1 cup brown sugar*

Melt the butter and scrape it into a medium-size bowl to cool. Melt the chocolate separately, then scrape it into another medium-size bowl to cool. Stir the white sugar into the chocolate until smooth.

Line a 10″ x 14″ cake or roasting pan with a double thickness of wide aluminum foil. Make sure you press the foil into the corners without tearing it. Grease the foil well. Preheat the oven to 350 degrees.

Stir the baking powder and vanilla into the butter, then the eggs. Beat it until smooth. Stir in the flour just until mixed. Remove 1¼ cups of the batter and stir it into the chocolate mixture until smooth. Stir the brown sugar into the remaining white batter.

Using a soup spoon, drop the chocolate batter into the pan,

leaving spaces between the chocolate clumps. Fill the spaces with the other batter. Stick a thin knife into one end of the batter, and drag it through, flat side forward, in several rows. That swirls the batters without running them together. Bang the pan on the counter a couple of times to smooth the surface of the cake. If it's still lumpy, pat it smooth with damp hands. Bake 35 minutes, until a skewer inserted into some chocolate batter in the center comes out clean.

*Serves 8 people.*

## ONION "RINGS OF FIRE"

Spike was a real nice old geezer—the best—but even he found it hard to forgive Al's brothers Simon and Theodore after they gave him that hotfoot. Actually, I think he would have forgiven them if his memory had come back after the accident.

It wouldn't have been so bad, except that Spike had just fallen into a tub of lard, as usual—this was before he started sleeping in one to ease his back pain. And, of course, there was that new Varathane paint job on his artificial leg.

It might still have been almost O.K., except that he didn't discover the fire for a couple of minutes because he was trying to pull out the butcher knife that had fallen off the counter and pinned his other foot to the floor.

Just then the electricity blew, and all you could see was a ring of fire as he desperately hobbled faster and faster while the flames grew higher and higher. It was so hot the bottles of hot sauce on the shelf above his head exploded. Drenching Spike and fueling the fire, the sauce inundated the bucket of onion ring batter that he was trying to shelter from the flames with his torn, bleeding body.

Miraculously the batter was saved—though Spike didn't look too good for a couple of years—and another masterpiece was created.

> *1 large egg yolk*
> *½ cup milk*
> *2 garlic cloves, put through a garlic press*
> *⅜ teaspoon ground thyme*
> *½ teaspoon baking powder*
> *¼ teaspoon salt*
> *¼–½ teaspoon ground hot chilies (Spike could*
>     *never face hot sauce again)*
> *2 tablespoons grated Parmesan cheese*
> *¼ cup yellow cornmeal*

*6 tablespoons white flour*
*Wesson oil*
*2 small-medium white or yellow onions*
*Heated spicy barbecue sauce*

Mix together the egg yolk, milk, and garlic with a fork in a medium-size bowl. Stir in the thyme, baking powder, salt, and chilies. Mix together the Parmesan, cornmeal, and flour, then stir that into the bowl with the fork.

Cover the batter with plastic wrap and refrigerate it. Pour enough oil into a large skillet to come up about 2″ high and turn the heat to high. Slice the onions ¼″–½″ thick, depending on how you like them. Separate them into rings.

When the oil's very hot (Spike said 375 degrees; I say very hot) but not smoking, turn the heat down to medium. Drop a few rings into the batter. Lift them out with a fork, letting the extra batter drip back into the bowl. Drop about 8 rings into the oil and fry, turning as needed, until they're browned. It only takes 2 minutes per batch. Drain on paper towels while you make the rest of the rings, in batches of 8. Serve them with the barbecue sauce.

*Serves 4 people.*

## "HOUND DOGS"

Spike's wife never had time to listen to him at home—between the day-care center and that specialty mail-order photo business she was putting in 19-hour days. So anytime we went to Johnny's we could be sure we'd hear one of Spike's great stories.

One day he was telling us about the time Rock Hudson came into Johnny's to use the men's room. Well, Spike was really getting into the story, acting out all the parts, and all the time he was wielding his cleaver like an artist as he carved up a rack of ribs with blinding speed. Of course he was nearly blind by now anyway, ever since the time he looked at the eclipse through a piece of smoked turkey. He said it was worth it—he saw God, but God didn't see him, which was the ideal situation. Well anyway, he had just gotten to the part of the story where old Rabbi Feldman comes tearing out of the men's room, and we thought Spike's screams were just something he was acting out.

They weren't. Somehow that sweet old man had managed to hack off his finger, which skidded across the counter, and into the deep-fryer. The next thing we knew, Connie, Spike's star waitress, absent-mindedly slapped the crisp golden-brown cylinder onto a bun. Spike kept trying to grab it away from her, but she thought he was just adding ketchup. Connie served it to a Swedish exchange student, and everyone crowded around Inga to watch her eat her first American hot dog. She loved it!

We all got together and threw Spike a party when he got out of the hospital. Of course it didn't cost us very much, since we held it at Johnny's and used Spike's food. The pièce de résistance was a new menu item, deep-fried hot dogs. Spike was so overwhelmed, he backed into a baloney slicer. I guess it was his way of saying thanks.

Just a couple of notes. The slashes in the hot dog let it cook all the way through, so the whole thing is even crisper than the original version. Slashed dogs are also great grilled, as long as you keep mashing them down with a spatula so they get really black.

*Wesson oil*
*2 hot dogs per person*

Heat about 1″ of oil in a skillet large enough to hold twice as many hot dogs as you're cooking. It should be so hot that a piece of bread or cigarette butt dropped into it begins sizzling right away. While it's heating, make a couple of diagonal slashes through one side of your hot dog about ¼ of the way through. Turn the hot dog over and make 2 more slashes going the other way. Put the hot dogs in the oil and cook until crispy brown all over, turning them often. They expand and become all twisted, but they're great.

# "WE CAN PORK IT OUT" SLOPPY JOSÉS

José was Spike's health inspector, and he and Spike used to always kid around. José would say, "Be sure you cook that pork all the way through." And Spike would josh, "Why don't you taste it and see?"

You should have seen the crowds at José's funeral. And afterward, as we always did in times of grief, we gathered at Johnny's where Spike introduced this dish in memory of a real professional and a great pal.

> *1 tablespoon olive or vegetable oil*
> *12 ounces spicy pork sausage meat*
> *28-ounce can + 14½-ounce can whole to-*
> *matoes, drained, roughly chopped*
> *1 medium onion, roughly chopped*
> *½ teaspoon dried oregano*
> *½ teaspoon dried mint*
> *Crushed black pepper to taste*
> *½ pound shredded soft white cheese like queso*
> *fresco or mozzarella or Monterey Jack*
> *6–7 large handfuls tortilla chips—the good kind,*
> *crushed if very big*

Heat the oil in a skillet over medium heat, add the sausage and fry until cooked through. Take the sausage out with a slotted spoon and put it in a sieve to drain.

Add the tomatoes, onion, oregano, mint, and pepper to the skillet and stir. Cover and cook 20 minutes, stirring 2 or 3 times.

Uncover the skillet and stir in the sausage, then the cheese. Stir until the cheese is melted, then fold in the chips and serve immediately.

*Serves 4 people.*

# "NEVER CAN'T SAY GOOD FRIES"

Don't get excited. These aren't those legendary fries that made Al "The Pig" Bundy a household name. Al's were just plain old all-American fries, the kind that glide down your throat when you're clocked at 64 per minute.

These are those other fries, the recipe Spike won off that guy from Cincinnati who came into the diner one day to place a big bet on the Cubs. It's kind of like that Cincinnati 5-way chili that East Coast food snobs make pilgrimages for. In Ohio they use spaghetti—which is O.K. if you have no taste—instead of fries. No wonder they call it Cincinnati.

Unfortunately, Spike's mind was fading in and out a little in those days (it was right after he'd been locked in accidentally over the weekend by the exterminators), so he forgot to place the bet. The Cubs won by 10.

Spike still liked the recipe, even after a couple of the guy's friends came back and sawed off one of his ears. "It was my bad ear," Spike would joke in one of the few later years that were left to him, "at least it is now." Luckily we didn't have to pay any attention to him, since he never did learn to read lips.

*50 French fries*
*3½ ounces Velveeta (about ½ cup)*
*½ cup chili with no beans*
*Cooked red kidney beans (optional, especially if I'm serving this to Al)*
*Finely chopped onions*

Fry the fries. Melt the Velveeta. Heat the chili and beans. Serve the fries topped with everything else. If you leave out one ingredient, it's 4-way fries. If you leave out two ingredients, it's 3-way fries. If you leave out any more, go eat some tofu, pal.

*Serves 2 people.*

# SUNDAE BUNDY SUNDAE

Spike was real excited when the diner got chosen as a polling place in the 1976 election. Things went fine all day, and Spike was ecstatic about the turnout. Eat, vote, eat, vote, eat, vote— I almost burst. At the end of the day, Spike insisted on treating everyone still there to a real gutbuster.

He brought out a whole "Devil or Angel" Cake topped with the greatest sundae he had ever made. He set it down and went inside the booth to vote. Twenty minutes later, when we dragged him out, he was still yelling, "Operator, give me back my dime!" When he recovered from his stroke, he found a letter waiting for him from the Carter campaign thanking him for his 10-cent contribution.

Of course in those 20 minutes, Al had completely demolished Spike's special sundae. So this is the only menu item that isn't named after a song. It's named after my Al, and nobody, even me, can take that away from him. When Spike got back from rehab, the menus were already printed and there wasn't anything he could do about it.

> 1 recipe "Devil or Angel" Cake (page 88)
> 2½ cups miniature marshmallows
> 1¾ cups walnut halves or pieces (6-ounce bag)
> 2–3 cups good butterscotch sauce
> 6 flavors of ice cream, 4 scoops of each
> 1 recipe "Black Is Black" Hot Fudge Sauce
>     (next recipe)
> Sweetened whipped cream or Reddi-whip
> Maraschino cherries (optional)

Leave the room temperature cake in the pan. Scatter the marshmallows and nuts on top in an even layer. Spread the butterscotch sauce over them. If you want, you can go ahead and make butterscotch sauce (page 10), or you can do what Spike did—buy it in bulk. The cake can be stored like this for several days at room temperature.

When you're ready to serve it, top with the ice cream. You should have 4 rows, each with 1 scoop of each flavor. At Johnny's you ordered "the sundae," which was the whole thing, or a double (a piece with 2 flavors of ice cream), triple (3 flavors), etc.

The fudge, whipped cream, and cherries were always served on the side so the fudge wouldn't melt the ice cream. The service was always very slow at Johnny's.

*Serves 1–24 people.*

## "BLACK IS BLACK" HOT FUDGE SAUCE

*1 stick unsalted butter, roughly chopped*
*6 tablespoons light corn syrup*
*1 cup white sugar*
*1 cup unsweetened cocoa, preferably Dutch*
    *process*
*1 cup heavy cream*
*2 teaspoons vanilla extract*

Melt the butter and corn syrup in a medium-size skillet over low heat. Stir in the sugar until smooth, then the cocoa, mashing any lumps. Turn the heat to medium-low. Stir in the cream until very smooth, then stir occasionally until it just comes to a boil. Immediately take it off the heat. Pour into a gravy boat and cool 5 minutes. Stir in the vanilla and serve.

You can make it in advance and store it in a wide-mouth jar in the refrigerator, but it becomes the texture of fudge when it's cold. Reheat just the amount you want over very low heat, stirring constantly.

*Makes 3 cups.*

I suppose you've realized by now that Al found out about the book. I think the kids sold me out for a trip to Fat Burger.

Al's idea of helping out in the kitchen is standing around saying, "What time is dinner rearing its ugly head?" Who knew he could cook? Anyway, here's Al's All-Man Beer 'N' Buns Dinner. If you don't tell your husband that fish is an aphrodisiac, then maybe he'll make this for you.

## BEER BATTER FISH WITH TATER BALLS

Al Bundy here. Unlike my powderpuff neighbor Steve, who won't scratch himself till Marcy tells him where it itches, I like food that fights back. Nothing beats the thrill of vanquishing a wild creature, once strong, noble, and free, now squirming on your hook, yearning to be released from the hell his life has become. Yeah, I guess that fish and me are a lot alike.

   *2 boiling potatoes, rinsed but not peeled*
*½ cup pre-sifted flour*
*¼ cup cornmeal*
*¾ teaspoon garlic salt + more for the potatoes*
*⅛ teaspoon black pepper*
*½ cup Budweiser, warm and flat*
 *1 large egg*
*2 teaspoons Wesson oil + more for frying*
*½ pound whitefish fillets*

Cut the potatoes into tiny little balls using a metal melon baller. Put them in an old coffee can and fill it with cold water from the creek. Mix together the flour, cornmeal, garlic salt, and pepper in the hubcap of a '57 Chevy using a clean stick. Don't scratch that hubcap—it's a classic. Twist an empty Bud can in half and pour in the flat beer, the egg, and the 2 teaspoons of oil. Cover the can with your hand and shake it to mix it up. Now stir it into the flour. Put the batter in your cooler while you catch those fish.

If all you get are fish the size of your bait, cook them whole. Or cook the bait, it really doesn't matter. If you get some real fish, cut the skinned fillets into pieces about 2″ x ½″ x ¼″. Heat about an inch of oil in a large pot over your fire until it's very hot. While it's heating, pour the water off the potatoes and dry them on your undershirt. Put about ¼ of the fish into the batter and stir them around with a stick so they get covered completely. Use the sharp end of the stick to pick the pieces up and toss them into the oil. They're ready in 2 or 3 minutes, when they're brown. Eat them now or they'll get soggy.

Fry the potatoes while you're eating the fish. Put ¼ of the balls into the hot oil. Stir them if they stick together, until they're brown. It takes about 4–5 minutes till they're done. Sprinkle on some garlic salt and eat them while you cook the other 3 batches.

*Serves 2 guys.*

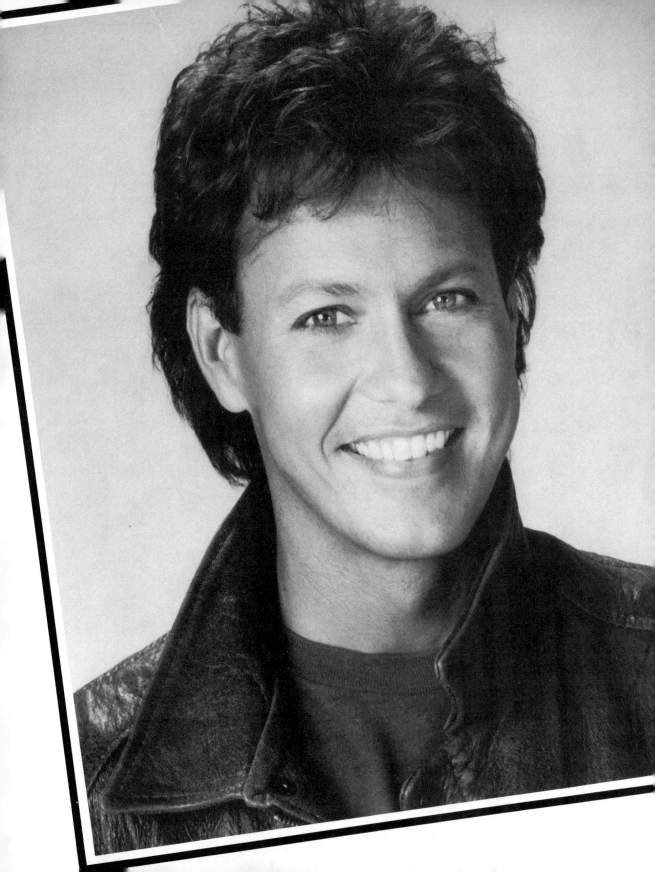

Final Bundy Bonus—From the Kitchen of Chef Boy R. Dees

Rick Dees, KIIS-FM radio personality and "King of the L.A. Airwaves" with his nationally syndicated "Rick Dees Weekly Top Forty," has made this special contribution, truly icing on the cake.

## DEES' CHOCOLATE, CHOCOLATE, CHOCOLATE CAKE

*1 package chocolate cake mix with pudding in
    the mix*
*¾ cup mayonnaise*
*¼ cup real butter*
*1 cup water*
*3 eggs*
*½ cup semi-sweet chocolate bits*

Grease and flour two 9″ layer cake pans. Use *real* butter to grease pans. In a large bowl, blend all ingredients, except for chocolate bits, with mixer on slow speed for 30 seconds. Then beat at medium speed for 2 minutes (or 300 strokes by hand). Pour ½ cup semi-sweet chocolate bits into batter. Pour into prepared pans. Bake in oven at 350 degrees for 35 minutes, or until cake pulls away from the sides of pans, and springs back when touched lightly in the center. Cool for 10 minutes. Remove and frost with Dees' Killer Frost (recipe follows).

## DEES' KILLER FROST

*½ cup hot water*
*4 squares of unsweetened chocolate*
*3 cups confectioner's sugar*
*3 egg yolks*
*½ cup soft butter (be sure to use real butter)*
*1 tablespoon vanilla extract*

Melt chocolate over hot water, or in microwave. In a medium bowl, combine chocolate, sugar, and ½ cup hot water. With electric mixer on medium speed, beat until smooth and well combined. Add egg yolks, butter, and vanilla. Continue beating until frosting is thick. Set the bowl in ice water, or in the refrigerator for 10 minutes. Frost that cake!!! Don't forget to frost the middle! It's DEESlicious!

# BIOGRAPHICAL NOTES
## The Writer
## Linda Merinoff:
## The Long Version

I know you're wondering how it happened . . . how a successful writer and journalist sinks so low as to collaborate with Peggy Bundy on a cookbook. It was a long, slow road to oblivion, so listen to my story and beware. It could happen to you!

I had a normal childhood, went to Antioch College, even attended some grad school—the Royal College of Art, School of Film and Television, in England. I began writing for rock & roll magazines while in school and became a columnist for one of the English weekly rock papers. Then, I hit the big time. I spent a summer working at *Cosmopolitan* magazine as a secretarial floater.

From there it was straight up. I interviewed smart, sexy men for *Penthouse*. I covered the U.S. Open Tennis Tournament, wrote about collecting art, interviewed the rich and famous. What could be better?

But I was bored. I realized that I had spent years of school training for a higher calling, and it was time to fulfill my destiny. I went to work for a TV network.

Sure, most people think being a television censor is all champagne and naked bodies. But it's much more. You spend hours talking to TV writers and producers. You write long memos and copy everyone in the company. You go to videotape and film locations and give everyone the benefit of your many years of experience, then bask in their appreciation knowing full well they wish they'd never hear from you again.

You'd think I'd be satisfied with all that . . . but once again I felt the need to spread my wings.

I left the network and went to work for Rona Barrett, producing her daily radio show. Motion picture premieres, private movie screenings, the Oscars, the Emmys, people returning my phone calls immediately—yes, this was the Hollywood I'd always dreamed about.

But something in my soul cried out for more. Frantically, I searched for my true destiny until one night I had a dream. "Write about food," a little voice said to me. I awoke with renewed hope and fervor, and began to write about food.

*The Glorious Noodle: A Culinary Tour Around the World* (Poseidon Press/Simon & Schuster) was my first published book. The critics raved. *Time* magazine called it one of the ten best cookbooks of the year.

*The Savory Sausage: A Culinary Tour Around the World* (Poseidon Press/Simon & Schuster) was next and met with an equally enthusiastic reception.

Then came *Gingerbread* (Fireside/Simon & Schuster—available at your bookstore now, only $8.99 plus tax). I thought I was immortal. I could do no wrong.

THEN CAME BUNDY.

I was shopping one day in a deserted mall. It was close to Halloween and I was looking for a hooker costume. I saw a shoe store filled with the tackiest merchandise imaginable, so I went in.

Just as I was about to sit down, the woman who was stealing money from the cash register emerged from behind the counter and sidled out the door. I ran after her. "Wait," I cried. "Wait! I'll give you $50 for your clothes." She stopped. "Make it $75 and they're yours." "Fine, if you throw in some lessons on how you walk."

We went to Fat Jack's Liver & Brew to close the deal. I don't know whether it was something she put in the drink she insisted I order (that one with the tiny umbrella), but just before I blacked out I'd agreed to write her book.

When I came to the next day, I tried to back out of the deal, but it seems I'd signed this little piece of paper. Oh, well, it looked like my signature, but at the time I was still too bleary-eyed to tell.

That was 14 months ago . . . it seems like a lifetime. I'm writing this from Happy Acres Sanitarium. You see, I had to spend the better part of a year in the belly of the beast—12 miserable months in the House of Bundy.

But don't worry, I'm going to be fine. Group therapy's not so bad. Besides, the doctors say it's only a matter of time before my appetite returns. I'm sure it will! I know it will!!

AS GOD IS MY WITNESS, ONE DAY I'LL BE HUNGRY AGAIN!!!

# The Writer
# Linda Merinoff:
# The Short Version

Linda Merinoff is a food writer who never thought she'd sink so low.

# The Bundy Family

## AL BUNDY

Al Bundy resides in Chicago, Ill., where he juggles his dual roles as professional and family man. Employed by Gary's Shoes and Accessories for Today's Woman, Bundy describes this challenging career as "minimum-wage-slow-death."

A devoted husband and father, Bundy spends his spare time ogling women, watching sports on TV and drinking beer. His other interests include ogling women, watching sports on TV and drinking beer.

Bundy's long-range plans include slow death by middle-class existence, which he hopes will deliver him from his self-inflicted living hell.

## PEGGY BUNDY

Peg Bundy is the consummate wife and mother. Dedicated entirely to her home and family, Peggy would rather die than work outside the home. She would rather die than work inside the home, too, but that's where her creative homemaking comes in handy.

Peg's culinary expertise is equaled only by her crafty consumerism. Many of her dollar-saving recipes are featured in this cookbook. Family favorites include "Bitch Cake," "Smoke Alarm Steak" and "Chernobyl Chicken Meltdown Sandwich."

An adamant supporter of the local arts scene, Peggy is personally responsible for generous contributions to Troy's male exotic dancers and Dial-a-Hunk.

Other interests include browbeating Al into the occasional romantic encounter, guiding and nurturing her children so that they don't follow in their father's pathetic footsteps and avoiding next-door-nerds Steve and Marcy Rhoades.

## KELLY BUNDY

Kelly Bundy, daughter of Al and Peggy Bundy, is a Chicago-area high school student with high aspirations. One day she even hopes to graduate.

In the meantime, Kelly is best known for her rapport with the opposite sex—teachers, students, janitors. In fact, just about any-one. A total lack of discrimination is one of Kelly's many endearing charms.

Blonde and beautiful, she's every man's dream and every mother's nightmare. Except her mother, Peg, who is proud as punch to have passed on her own rigorous moral standards to her daughter.

But lovely Kelly is bright enough to learn from her mother's mistakes. She plans to eventually bag some rich guy and get the hell out of the Bundy household.

## BUD BUNDY

Though only a high-schooler, young Bud has distinguished himself as a sensitive and caring member of the Bundy clan. He frequently takes time out from his busy schedule to tutor his dullard sister, Kelly, in her schoolwork. The fact that his teachings resemble the plots of old television series doesn't diminish the fact that he cares deeply enough to lie through his teeth.

Bud's social life is as dull as his academic life is bright. But Kelly is always there to remind him that although he may never get a date, he'll always have a pillow named Shirley.

# The Rhoades

## MARCY RHOADES

Former manager of Kyoto National Bank, perky Marcy Rhoades refuses to let recent personal and professional set-backs get her down. Demoted to the humiliating position of drive-up window teller after covering husband Steve's bad loan to neighbor Al Bundy, Marcy is determined to start her climb back up the corporate ladder.

Under Marcy's dress-for-success exterior lies a seething sexuality. But with her marriage on a rocky road, Marcy has been forced to discover the kinky comforts of a shower massage.

Although her career and home life may not be all she desires, Marcy has only to look next door to take comfort in one unshakable fact—she's not a Bundy.

## STEVE RHOADES

Steve Rhoades is a former banking professional who has decided to jump off the fast-paced merry-go-round of big business in order to find the simpler, soul-nourishing existence that he so desperately craves and so richly deserves. The fact that he got fired and can't even keep a menial, minimum-wage job only serves to confirm his conviction that he is, at long last, on the right career path.

Although his ambitious wife, Marcy, finds the entire situation deplorable and considers her husband's fall from fiduciary grace an intolerable embarrassment, she stands by her man through thick and thin. Except, of course, when he's off visiting his mother.

Since lowering both his professional and personal standards, Rhoades has come to appreciate the Bundy's slovenly ways. Their next-door-neighbor for several years, Steve is practically a member of the Bundy family.